The Psychedelic Chalice:

Tales from the Aussie Underground

by

Dale Carruth

Title: The Psychedelic Chalice: Tales from the Aussie Underground

Author: Dale Carruth

Published by 3 Feathers Books

3feathersbooks@gmail.com

3feathers3@protonmail.com

Cover Art by Dale Carruth

Proofreading and editorial advice:

ISBN: 9780645324952 print

ISBN: 9780645324969 ebook

Subjects: Underground Psychedelic Therapy – Psychedelic Therapy - Healing Trauma – Psychotropic Drugs – Entheogens – Psychedelics – Plant Medicines – MDMA – Psilocybin Mushrooms – Ayahuasca – Iboga – DMT – 5MeODMT - Australia - Underground

First Edition, March 2024.

Printed by Ingram Spark

The Psychedelic Chalice:

Tales from the Aussie Underground

by

Dale Carruth

Other Publications by Dale Carruth and Awards

2022 – Transformations: Healing Trauma with Psychedelic Therapy.

2021 – Beating the Benzo Blues: Getting off Benzodiazepines.

2018 – 2024 -12 Psychedelic Therapy Feature Articles

2000 – 2021 - Some forty feature articles published in various magazines.

2004 – Award; Creative NZ-PEN Manuscript Assessment.

2003 – Award: Creative NZ-PEN Mentorship.

Contents

"Alienation from nature and the loss of the experience of being part of the living creation is the greatest tragedy of our materialistic era. It is the causative reason for ecological devastation and climate change. Therefore, I attribute absolute highest importance to consciousness-change. I regard psychedelics as catalyzers for this. They are tools which are guiding our perception toward other, deeper, areas of human existence, so that we, again, become aware of our spiritual essence. Psychedelic experiences in a safe setting can help our consciousness open up to this sensation of connection and of being one with nature. LSD and related substances are not "drugs" in the usual sense, but are part of the sacred substances which have been used for thousands of years in ritual settings." — **Albert Hoffmann**

Acknowledgements

I thank Mother Nature for the entheogenic plants, frogs and fungi and for freely bestowing their healing powers upon us.

I thank all the underground facilitators who bravely took part in this book.

I thank my mentors; Julian Palmer and Friederike Meckel Fischer for your ongoing support and advice.

I thank anyone who campaigns for the legalization of psychedelic and entheogenic medicines.

I thank all the podcasters and youtubers who freely provide psychedelic information.

I thank my friend and spiritual sister Donna Ross Tiegan for your ongoing and unwavering friendship and support.

I pay tribute to my traumatised friends who never made it, and my inspirational friends and mentors who have passed on to a better place.

I pay tribute to the psychedelic elders who have paved the way and the people who have been wrongly incarcerated as a result of trying to heal themselves or help others heal with psychedelics and entheogens.

Introduction

"The Underground," the very words evoke images of shady characters, dodgy dealers, law breakers, slick operators, and dark web shenanigans – and in this age of the so called, "2nd Psychedelic Renaissance," some may well have vested interests in painting such a sordid picture of Australia's underground psychedelic healers. But please do understand – it's only the "2nd psychedelic renaissance" for those who actually stopped using them!

Psychedelics were once legal and used with astounding success to heal a host of mental health disorders in the 40s 50s and 60s. After they were demonized and banished by the powers that be - the bravest of apostles, convinced of their immense healing and spiritual benefits, just quietly shut a door on society and carried on. Others, who later experienced their astounding healing benefits, rose up like phoenixes to join them.

Despite the misinformation and controversy that banished psychedelics from mainstream medicine for the past fifty odd years, their healing potential is once again being enthusiastically espoused in the media and research universities around the world are studying them. After years of emphatic resistance, suddenly out of the blue, the land of Oz – Australia, became one of the first countries in the world to legalise MDMA and psilocybin mushrooms for therapeutic use.

Australia is currently in the process of introducing MDMA and psilocybin into legal mainstream medicine for the healing of a multitude of mental health disorders. However, please don't get too excited as this is looking to be a tightly controlled process, with stringent entry criteria, and an exorbitant cost to potential recipients. One woman I recently spoke to was quoted a staggering $25,000 for a series of three MDMA treatments, including some requisite counselling. This estimate came via Mind Medicine Australia. I'm grateful that MMA rallied vigorously for the legalising of psychedelics on a mandate that espoused them as an urgently needed therapeutic treatment for mental health disorders – but three MDMA sessions, with counselling, costs approximately one-tenth of that in the underground.

Glaringly absent from the mainstream conversations to date, are the voices and wisdom of the experienced underground practitioners who have been administering psychedelic potions to Australians for at least the past twenty-five years. Yes, underground psychedelic therapy is alive and well and has operated, largely with impunity, across Australia for years. So, at this pivotal time, with science and capitalism dominating the dialogue, and the voices of wisdom and experience being ignored, I sensed the real importance of documenting the stories of some of Australia's underground healers.

While this book constitutes just a small cross section of those involved, it is, in my opinion, a representative sample of the people you are likely to encounter in the Australian psychedelic underground. It includes several practitioners who were present at the inception of the Western ayahuasca movement in Australia, in the mid-90s.

The practitioners, whose stories you are about to read, bring a depth of knowledge and wisdom to the psychedelic conversation that is pretty much essential to informing the way forward. They also constitute some of the real heroes of the psychedelic renaissance, as they have been, (and some still are,) committed to providing much needed healing to the traumatized people lucky enough to find them - despite great legal risk to themselves.

The people who facilitate this healing are variously trained - employing a range of methods, from traditional Peruvian Shamanism, to self-taught, psychotherapeutic and plant-spirit guided. All have conducted this healing within Australia, and represent the vast melting pot of cultures that make up the population: Russian, German, New Zealander, South African, English, Chinese, and Australian.

The space of the Australian underground psychedelic ceremony is vast - both in relation to the medicines administered and the way in which healing is conducted. Ayahuasca, Iboga, 5-MeO-DMT, Psilocybin mushrooms, MDMA, Mescaline Cactus and Kambo - each offer their own unique healing profiles and all are covered in this book.

Note: This book does not attempt to cover indigenous plant medicine practices. While it's important to acknowledge that they do exist, they remain a largely oral and secretive tradition and hence outside the scope of this book.

Some Australian Plant Medicine History.

Nick Space Tree and Darpan were among the first to start experimenting with Acacia brews in the Northern Rivers region of New South Wales. While Nick Space Tree has become a bit of a recluse (I'm told), and is unlikely to talk on record - Darpan is still an active and a somewhat iconic figure in the psychedelic community.

Introduced to LSD and mushrooms in the early seventies whilst studying Psychology at Flinders University, he quickly became a psychedelic convert after realising their immense healing potential. He was deeply influenced by the work of Dr Stanislav Grof, a pioneer in the use of psychedelics in Psychiatry, so after graduating with honours he received further training at a Dutch university where he was instructed in the use of MDMA within a therapeutic context. It was not until his mid-forties that Darpan's interest in ayahuasca was sparked. He was involved in an ayahuasca study group and in 1996, the group ambitiously decided to invite infamous American psychonaut, Terence Mckenna to Australia. Against all expectations, Mckenna agreed, citing an abiding interest to visit, "The land of the Acacias."

Mckenna bought with him forbidden fruit from his ethnobotanical garden – including one of Australia's first ayahuasca vines. His first stop was Byron Bay, where he gave a series of lectures and delivered an unforgettable psychedelic rap at the legendary "Beyond the Brain" Festival. He then went on to do a lecture tour of the major cities. Terence became firm friends with Darpan and began sending him regular shipments of Hawaiian made Ayahuasca for his personal use. After this initiation, Darpan was inspired to travel to Ecuador, Peru and Brazil to train with a number of Shamans. Meanwhile he began to hold some of Australia's first ayahuasca ceremonies. He later trained others, passing on his knowledge to those who felt the call.

Darpan was also the first person in Australia to get arrested for possession of Ayahuasca (DMT) He says that this incident was like a rite of passage. After a year of house arrest and the subsequent court case, the charges were dismissed. He believes that the plant spirits were testing him, guiding the process and ultimately watching over him. When you consider that his legal fees were funded by a wealthy client - and his bail, (set at $350,000) was posted by another - this seems entirely feasible.

Until recently he travelled annually to Europe speaking at conferences and facilitating shamanic retreats. He has pioneered the use of Ayahuasca within a ceremonial context in both Europe and Australia opening new pathways which are now well established.

Julian Palmer, who's story features in this book, is another dedicated provider of psychedelic sacraments. Iconic, irreverent, and a lover of controversy, Julian is a vocal public figure in the Australian psychedelic underground. He has written a book, spoken at international entheogenic conferences and festivals, and featured on various television programmes. Following close on Darpan's heels, he and his mate, Dan Shreiber, (now deceased) surfed the web to gather intel on scared plant potions. They began concocting and trialling different acaciahuasca brews, and later began serving it to groups in 2001. The Ozzie version of ayahuasca, is often referred to as Acaciahuasca because several native DMT containing acacias are used in the brew.

Julian's motivation to serve the brew was inspired by the positive results he saw in the people who drank it. Serving it freely for seven and a half years, at 3 to 6 gatherings a year - he only began charging in 2009. He also taught others to make the acacia tea and over the years, has helped many Aussie facilitators in a variety of practical ways – myself included.

Of course, there would be no facilitation of Ayahuasca without the Amazonian vine, Banisteriopsis Caapi. The story of the first vine smuggled into Australia is told to me by Col Hawk, whose story also features in this book. A man we will refer to as 'M' had gotten his hands on a book about toxic plants from the library when he was still in Primary school. He was fascinated with a section at the back about Amazonian snuff practices. This fascination turned into an obsession and he saved up money from odd jobs. At the tender age of 17, he took himself off to the Amazon and lived with a tribe for a month.

He sampled a few different ayahuasca vines, but the Shamans told him if he was going to smuggle just one, to take the Cielo Vine as it is the best allrounder. So, M bought back an unrooted cutting wrapped in sphagnum moss in his tooth brush container. He raised it in a pot until he could finally get it in the ground in 1996. It grew to a monster, the largest vine anyone has seen. Hundreds of lives have been transformed by it and its clones. M also bought back seeds for a whole range of Mescaline Cactus, that are now the Australian Standard in most entheogenic collectors gardens.

It was around this same time 96/97, that McKenna bought over his vine and John Seed, another psychedelic elder from The Rainforest Alliance, was given a cutting of an Ecuadorian vine by the great Shaman, Cosimera, for saving his rainforest and vine habitat from loggers. It is still thriving in the Northern Rivers and is a vine that has a real psychic component to it, if you properly connect to its 'agency.'

The group that has really informed the Australian Psychedelic community was the Shaman Australis Forum (SAB.) A pre social media internet forum where people shared information, plants, trip reports and their lives. There is also an associated nursery selling legal plants, herbs and books. They later started meeting in person, forming deep friendships, alliances, and community. A couple of organisations were later birthed from this group.

The first was Entheogenesis Australia (EGA) established in 2004 and according to Hawk one of the best psychedelic hubs in the world. Its conferences attract the legends of psychedelics and plant medicines from around the world, including the likes of Rick Doblin (MAPS), Kathleen Harrison, Dennis McKenna and Graham Hancock. The conferences started in 2010 and were foundational in the establishment of this scene. These conferences were world class and EGA was a dynamic cultural movement with its fair share of politics, unique characters and Australian cultural influences. In 2013, EGA launched a YouTube video channel - Entheo TV - enabling the public free access to the educational material recorded at EGA conferences.

PRISM (Psychedelic Research in Science and Medicine) started in 2010. Then came The Australian Psychedelic Society, that now has chapters in most states. The APS holds regular meetings which include; presentations of psychedelic movies, speakers, information sessions and social meet ups. They also advocate for the legalisation of psychedelics.

So, Australia has an active hub of informed elders who have been self-policing this community for many years. The anecdotal evidence from this community, exploring plant medicines for 20 plus years, is that the benefits are great, and the damage is rare, when using experienced facilitators. There has been very little injury by misadventure.

My previous book; Transformations: Healing Trauma with Psychedelic Therapy, 2021, was born out of my own experiences of navigating the underground as both a client and a therapist and a desire to keep the psychedelic medicine space safer, especially for traumatised people. It has a strong focus on educating underground facilitators how to work with traumatised people – e.g. how to conduct a thorough assessment, how to work with altered states of consciousness and the importance of providing follow up integration counselling.

Julian and Darpan are still going strong and are currently focused on recording their adventures and intel for posterity. Julian recently produced a psychedelic documentary (Contemplations on the Psychedelic Experience) and is currently writing another book. Many others have sprung up to join the underground medicine scene, offering various potions and differing degrees of experience, training, motivation, and integrity.

Consuming The Sacrament

To truly understand the exceptional power of entheogenic medicines, to not just heal trauma, but to elicit paradigm shattering spiritual experiences, one must first consume them. True understanding only begins with a willingness to submit ourselves to our own personal healing. In the underground this is deemed an absolute necessity before one even thinks about guiding others through such complex terrains and processes.

"Once people take these medicines, including psychologists and psychiatrists they cannot deny the reality of the spiritual "component.' So, this is the first requirement – to consume the sacrament." Chris Bache podcast.

It bears mentioning that the soon to be legal psychedelic therapists in Australia, generally have minimal if any experience taking these medicines – mainly because they are illegal and so can't be used in their training. MMA offer a breathwork session and call this an 'altered state of consciousness,' which it largely is, but bears little resemblance to the real deal. Yes, it's highly likely that a few of those training, have had some personal experiences with the medicines – but to send people out to work with clients in altered states of consciousness requires far more experience than one or two sessions.

Another topic almost absent from the current scientific and media discourse is that the transformative power of psychedelics goes far beyond the healing of trauma. These plants, fungi and frogs connect us to Mother Nature, and spirit realms. They offer a direct connection to God, Source, Spirit, Creative Intelligence; whichever term takes your fancy, and hence, will likely cause deep unrest in the sacrosanct halls of religion. The healing of mental health is just the start of the psychedelic conversation.

To the best of my knowledge, a book like this has never been written. These psychedelic wizards (and witches) of Oz, who between them have clocked up thousands of hours of immersive practice are about to reveal all and this book constitutes a rare and compelling distillation of their knowledge, insight, and experience. This is a source book of wisdom for future generations of psychedelic healers, and the many traumatised people seeking authentic healing and spiritual transformation, weather that be in the underground or through legal channels.

The 10 Apostles and their Forbidden Fruit.

Col Hawk – Ayahuasca, Acaciahuasca, Cactus

Skye Cielita Flor – Ayahuasca

Julian Palmer – Ayahuasca, Acaciahuasca, Changa, Cactus, MDMA

Juliana Wright – Iboga, Kambo

Spam Spagnoli – 5-MeO-DMT

Pip – Psilocybin Mushrooms

Nick S – Acaciahuasca, Kambo, Mescaline Cactus, Iboga

Yvonne S - Kambo.

Alex Korjavine - Cactus, Ayahuasca, Kambo, Changa

Dale C – MDMA, Psilocybin Mushrooms

Ten Psychedelic Apostles & the Forbidden Fruit

CHAPTER ONE

Col Hawk - Ayahuasca and Cactus.

My name is Hawk. I was born in 1960. My first childhood memories were of eating bitter Begonias and jumping off a small wall, pretending we could fly. Luckily, we didn't eat the poisonous Oleanders growing nearby. I grew up next to the largest and most gothic cemetery in the Southern hemisphere. It was a wonderland for little boys to play in. We often came across open tombs, vandalised by old vagrants, coffins looted for copper and bodies for gold teeth and jewellery. We dared each other to go inside to look at the skulls, another initiation which started my fascination with life and death. As a boy I read every book of ghost stories I could find and at age thirteen, I found a book on Tibetan mysticism. It was all about auras, astral travelling, and supernatural abilities.

I had my first LSD trip at sixteen years old. This was a total epiphany and I chased that dragon for many years and hundreds of trips. My gardening journey started with growing screening plants to disguise my weed. Then after reading books by Carlos Castaneda and Timothy Leary, and a few other publications, I became aware of these 'other' plants – plants I had no access to. But along came the internet which provided easy access to the sourcing of these medicine plants and this changed the whole game.

In 2000 I watched a show on Ayahuasca on SBS and wondered why I didn't know about this. Within a fortnight - thanks to the internet - I had the raw materials. I had them sent from an ethnobotanic supplier in London. Then I just happened to meet the best-connected guy and got some cuttings from a Caapi (ayahuasca) vine and then all the mescaline cactuses. He also had mushrooms and crystal DMT, so I went on an instant and very steep learning curve.

I drank my first ayahuasca brew by myself in the garden and it certainly eclipsed all those LSD experiences. The next ten years were spent experimenting - dosing myself and drinking brews with other brothers from the Shaman Australis forum. We were all doing the same thing - growing and learning about these plants.

After about ten years, people started doing public Ceremonies. I attended a cross section to suss out their brews and their styles. The first one I went to was a total trainwreck - too many people - too many freakouts. I stepped up and helped out. The facilitators were impressed and said I could join their crew. It was an apprenticeship of sorts - for five years, eight times a year doing retreats. We did Cactus one night, Ayahuasca the next. Twenty people at a time, all ages, nationalities, and dispositions.

I saw how these medicines affected this wide spectrum of people and how it served a social function - many great friendships were formed. Parents would bring their kids and kids would bring their parents. But what it really taught me, was that those large groups didn't really achieve maximal results. No matter how well you pre bonded as a group, there would always be some grandstander, some drama queen, some distraction, and disruption - a psychic soup of people losing their shit. People would come maybe a half a dozen times, or off and on for a couple of years, to achieve what should have been done, with proper help and guidance, in one night.

My apprenticeship with my vine took 15-years. It was a teacher and pupil relationship. Then one day it finally said that we were equals and that I could leave my day work and use it full time to support myself. We are a healing duo now. When my plants told me I could retire from my usual work and use them to heal others and to support myself, it was on the condition that I only do small groups and give personal guidance. My plants don't want to be wasted, they want to give optimal benefit, so I have done small weekly sessions for the last five years.

I see my work as a calling. My grandfather was a great gardener and a famous natural healer. I feel like I'm following in his footsteps. I'm sharing the attributes and benefits of my garden. I have the right set up, and the time is right to develop this great new marriage of the Vine and the Acacia, and share these secrets to those who are called to me.

I've received many testimonials from people whose lives have been changed, and now that those wheels are turning, why would I stop assisting people on these deepest of levels. That part is very satisfying - but if you thought it through, you would be crazy to do this work. It's certainly not glamorous; complete strangers losing their shit in your loungeroom - wrestling with and extracting people's demons - cleaning up puke. One night a lady even defecated everywhere - twice. It's a pretty crazy vocation.

I've been drinking and experimenting with Ayahuasca and Cactus for twenty years - ten years experimenting with myself and friends - five years assisting at group retreats - the last five years working full time as a plant-based healer. Whilst I occasionally facilitate a high dose mushroom journey, I mainly work with Cactus and Ayahuasca. I only work with plants that I grow myself and have a relationship with. I believe by raising and caring for plants, the nurture is built into the nature. My Ayahuasca vine is twenty years old. It has been my teacher. I have fed it and cared for it, now it cares for and supports both me and my clients. Whilst I did a couple of years of running Cactus retreats, I now mainly serve Ayahuasca. It's like being loyal to one partner and not having other plant mistresses.

Ayahuasca is a far more effective healing agent - almost dependable. And the most important factor is that we are evolving a whole new medicine here in Australia. Mother Ayahuasca has done her apprenticeship in the Amazon, and during my watch, has come to Australia to be with the great Acacia, the actual 'Tree of Knowledge'.

It's an incredible privilege to be an ambassador for this grand new union. My community has determined the most suitable Acacia species for this work and I've been shown Acacia secrets by the plants themselves. When the time is right, the medicine for that time presents itself.

The most important thing is that first-person relationship with your plants. To make your medicine from scratch. It starts by holding that seed in your hand and telling it; "You are going to be in my medicine, and heal many people." You care for the plant, how you would like it to care for your clients - you help it grow strong. I don't know how some facilitators can just source brew or ingredients and think that they can work with those plants that they have no relationship with.

I don't advertise or solicit for my business. People find me through my reputation and word of mouth recommendations. I work one on one with people who ask, otherwise I do small groups of either three women or three men, I will do four people if they are friends and are comfortable with each other. These small groups ensure everyone gets personal guidance and assistance.

During our pre session bonding there is time to drill down a bit into people's story and intentions. I can always assess who will be disruptive in a group; those with OCD or PTSD can get restless and noisy. I have a different business model to most, I don't encourage repeat visits. It's an initiation - I want them to dig deep. Most issues can be resolved in one good session. People can come once a year If they need. This is also about sustainability. I get around 150 doses a year from my plants so I want to help 150 different people, rather than have the same people coming over repeatedly. My plants ensure people get what they need, and also ensure their own longevity.

I feel that if somebody makes it through my front door, they are meant to be there. They have been called in by the plants. This is often confirmed when three random strangers complement each other perfectly. Sometimes someone might cancel but a fill in always appears, and that is usually perfect. The person who cancelled was not meant to be there and the new person will complement the energies better.

I adhere to standard practises of not working with schizophrenics or people with a history of psychosis, nor those on SSRI or SNRI anti-depressants. I try to make people feel comfortable in my home and they usually always open up to me, during the pre-dose meet and greet. The skeletons come out of the closet and people tell me things they've never told anyone else.

Another best practice protocol is that I never see lone woman - I organise a chaperone. Not because I don't trust myself, but because I have seen people dream up all sorts of reasons to keep their ego from being overpowered by the medicine. I wouldn't want that reason to be that someone imagined that I was being inappropriate.

The client stays overnight and we always have a good debriefing session the next morning. My integration is simple - just be kind – be kind to yourself, and all those you meet. Challenge yourself with acts of kindness. It puts you in the moment. I try to set an example, I could just simply dose people - give them an Ayahuasca experience to cross off their bucket list, but I do everything I can to get the optimum results - out of kindness. I tell people that they are free to contact me post session for assistance if they require it, but that rarely happens.

I work in my home 'temple', under the protection of my plants. The experience I offer is also about being with the plants, and the guy who is highly attuned to them. People usually arrive feeling quite nervous but after I show them around my garden the nerves seem to disappear, so that's the biggest drawback resolved. Hopefully they can see how healthy my plants are and my relationship with them, which on every level is part of my medicine. Everything I serve comes from my garden, and is nontoxic. I have complete control over the growing process.

I usually serve two doses of brew. I ease people in, assess their sensitivity to the brew. I don't believe in serving one big dose and throwing people in at the deep end. I believe that the facilitator needs to dose too, to be in the same space as the client and channel the wisdom of the plant and to understand the signposts from spirit - to work as equals.

I've witnessed some amazing transformations. In November 2020, I saw a young, aboriginal guy, a war veteran who'd served in Afghanistan. His intention was mainly to deal with his post war PTSD, but also to discover his lost Aboriginal heritage. He was a friend of my daughters, so I decided to give him some value-added extras. I took him up to

Mt Yengo, which is one of the most important aboriginal sacred sites in Australia. I showed him some of the rock carvings in the vicinity. These were the first he'd ever paid any attention to. I also decided to serve his ayahuasca on this sacred ancestral land. A week later, while he was out bushwalking, he discovered a partial rock carving and set about uncovering it. It may have been done by his great, great, great, great, great, great, great, grandfather. This was the medicine - fulfilling his noble intention to uncover his past.

He now works for the local Aboriginal Council as their Cultural Officer and is educating teachers and children alike. His passion is magnetic - but more importantly, he now has the Sacred Ceremonial duty to restore the Pictographs - including the one he discovered. He was given cultural authority to clean up around it and since then he has found associated carvings that tell the story of a comet strike 13,000 years ago. And with the guidance of the Elders, they have found and restored many other lost carvings in the area. This all happened because he connected to his heritage through Spirit - via the Acacia. And how great it is to have a brother who knows the secret, sacred and cultural art sites and of course - all these sacred sites are surrounded by Acacias.

I believe he will be the one chosen, to go to the restricted area on top of Mt Yengo, to download the new dreaming and songs. He feels it calling. But that may need a few more brews and a lot more cultural connection and authority. His personality and presence are such that, I think he will bridge and heal some of the rifts and politics within the Coastal Aboriginal groups. So, he certainly got his money's worth from the healing – and even got a job from it too. Such a top bloke. This is the power of this great new medicine. The activation of the Acacia with Ayahuasca is bringing magic back into the world. It was also a clear message to me, that this new medicine can activate the First Nations Peoples, Dreaming.

Another night - I sat under my vine with another war veteran client, who told me about some of the people he'd killed and the many friends he'd watched die in gore - blown to bits by bombs and landmines. He was practically nonverbal just five hours before, when he walked through my door. The trauma and PTSD he'd suffered from 30 years as a Special Forces operative and the taking of life, had unseated his spirits connection to his body. His soul was out of alignment. He was off the rails.

The medicine gave him a perfectly sequenced raft of psychic and mystical experiences, then dissolved his body like aspirin in water. His spirit left and he re-experienced his best friend's death - witnessed his mates spirit telling his destroyed body; "Its ok to stop breathing." He revisited and re framed his trauma from a spirit perspective, with Quantum time travel. He then re-birthed back into his body in correct alignment. He came back feeling lighter and healed.

All this was accessed and orchestrated entirely by plants. This is clearly far more effective than the many years of therapy these poor veterans receive at the taxpayers' expense. Tens of thousands of dollars are spent on each one of them, and none of them heal. Compared to 500 bucks and a cup of "tea" - one night of psychic surgery with a gardener. And I have to break the law to do this healing work that prevents suicide and saves the tax payers millions.

Another time, I was asked to help a lady who'd been addicted to ICE for years. She was associated with a drug related murder. Her mother was a high profile Australian, so it was all front-page news. Her innocence was later proven and she was released from jail but the demons were still attached to her, manifesting in Fibromyalgia, and a whole range of physical issues.

I gave her a private session that turned into a full-blown exorcism. I have powerful Tibetan skulls and exorcism daggers and I put them to full use. She purged out years of pain and regret. Her physical issues and fibromyalgia cleared up and her whole life changed. Her mother later invited me for tea and scones and thanked me profusely, saying that this was the best year of her life - to have gotten her daughter back. This is a good reminder that when people heal, it ripples out and effects their friends and family, and even human consciousness. We are close friends now and she currently works as an assistant to another facilitator who also features in this book.

But there are also challenging experiences. During COVID, I agreed to do a solo session with a chronically depressed guy. He had tried to commit suicide ten years prior, but was found, cut down, and revived. But he didn't fully return. He still had one foot in the spirit world. Psychically I could still see the noose around his neck. He was a big strong miner, and could have torn me apart. During the night he had a psychotic break. I was in a very dangerous situation. Luckily, I was able to calm him down, and we got some good healing done. We released negative energies and entities that had attached to him, then reconnected him back to Earth.

After that episode my medicine recently told me that I've paid my dues to depressed people. Send them to a suicide lifeline. It's not Ayahuasca's job to deal with the effects of modern society. There are legions of anxious and depressed people. Acacia told me that it's been waiting on its mountain for 15000 years to join with Ayahuasca and enter human consciousness. It's not the role of this medicine to give people a reason to live. It wants to expand consciousness. It seeks the .001% of people ready to ascend to a new level of perception, to awaken the divine. Consequently, I have started attracting less damaged people - people ready for awakening. I love it when I can take people to the next level, not just give them a reason to live.

My interaction with the client is always on a psychic level, Ayahuasca is about the "occult." The word "occult" means hidden. Usually, some secret that initiated adepts know how to apply. Everything about Ayahuasca is occult or hidden; the alkaloid hides in the plants, the combination of plants, the brewing method, all secrets that need to be shared and learnt. How to dose and guide people are all the skills of an adept who know these secrets. How to take people into other realms, and interpret their visions. Ayahuasca has its own secret methods, taking people through time and space, meeting the dead, all things termed supernatural.

My clients include psychiatrists and psychologists, who come to me to see what all the fuss is all about. I transform more lives every year, than most shrinks ever will in their whole career. Most issues are accumulations and aberrations of the fear-based Ego.

The nature of the physical is decay and corruption. I dissolve the filters and barriers between mind and the heart to reveal to people their Spirit - the full spectrum of their true nature and to embody that they are a powerful, sovereign, sentient being of light. Spirit cannot get cancer or PTSD or depression. Spirit is divine and incorrupt. When people see their issues, challenges, traumas as corresponding with the evolution of their soul - healing is achieved in a single session.

True healing is affected through Spirit, not the body. Ego is the fear-based system of the mind, which produces thought. Spirit is the love-based system of the heart which produces feelings. When in balance, love trumps fear. Feelings can be trusted, inner tuition followed, not feared, and dismissed by the thinking narrative, which wants to be in control, even if it makes you miserable. To be in divine awareness is to flip operating systems from Ego/fear to Heart/love.

Ok here is where we get to the part that might challenge my credibility. My day job is an Ayahuasca guy, but my spiritual practice is Tibetan Occultism. I started reading about this when I was 13. This is to do with things like auras and astral travelling. When I took that first acid trip, the main epiphany was I could see my etheric field, and I realised everything I had read about Tibetan mysticism was true. Then Tibetan religious relics started coming to me. I probably have Australia's largest collection of Tibetan skulls. These are the adorned and decorated skulls of high Lama, Tibetan saints. Thighbone trumpet, skull drum with human skin, and exorcism daggers, bells, and bowls etc. These are very powerful talismanic objects, with the providence of having been used in historical secret rituals by an elite class of monks.

I believe that through my skulls, I am in contact with the same interdimensional or ascended beings that the Tibetans were in contact with. In my private practice I drink Ayahuasca out of a skull bowl, and after many years and practice I am now a full initiate of that interdimensional lodge. These objects and my lodge connections make my space incredibly safe. You would have to get up pretty early in the morning, and have some pretty fancy kit to launch a psychic attack on me. Entities and psychic parasites take one look around and know that they are fucked. I'm not scared of anything, and can banish everything. I have a particular skull cap that is like a vacuum, it sucks unwanted energies out of people back to whence they came from. And of course, when people come to a Shamans house, they would be very disappointed if there weren't some skulls and occult bling everywhere.

What aspiring facilitators need to know is that they need to consume a lot of medicine. They need familiarity with the plants, how to prepare and dose them. They should have witnessed a lot of different people being dosed and see the wide range of reactions and responses.

I think a facilitator needs to be aged over 40 or 50, to have had a wide range of life experiences, worked hard, paid their dues to society, met all personality types in the process - raised a family, assisted aged parents, all those life experiences. An ayahuasca vine takes ten years to really make good medicine, and it takes a minimum of ten years dosing to make a good facilitator. How is a person in their 30's going to relate to a menopausal woman who has just watched her mother die from a protracted illness for example.

One needs to be very aware, sexually detached, mild tempered, have nerves of steel to be calm during the storm, good people skills, and be a fearless psychic surgeon. They should know that it's not glamourous – you're cleaning puke buckets, cleaning toilets, dealing with the panic of the inevitable fight or flight response. If you really sat down and thought about it, having people lose their shit, shed their entities, puke and scream in your loungeroom, who would want that? You also need to be humble - resisting all temptation to be a Guru, or seduce the vulnerable.

For people who want to sit with ayahuasca, there are several things they need to know: First; is that you need to have been "called." This is the start of the psychic process. Synchronicity and alignments are a key indicator that it's your time for the Medicine. Secondly; you need to check your suitability regarding medications you are taking or psychiatric conditions that may be contraindicated with the medicine. Thirdly; it's pointless going into an ayahuasca session if you are not prepared to surrender to the process – for if you fight this medicine, you definitely will not win. Fourthly; you need to carefully select your facilitator. They should have given you a good account of themselves and their experience, and be available and willing to answer your questions both before and after the session.

However, being informed is only good up to a point - you don't want to come with too many expectations. You cannot anticipate how and what will happen. Ayahuasca is definitely the master of blindsides. It will often address your intention and issues from a lateral perspective – one you could never have anticipated or imagined. But post session you will see that this was perfect.

My only fears around the work I do, are about the legality. There is nothing worse than the police invading your privacy and looking under every nook and cranny to find stuff to convict you for. If you grow your own plants, it's obvious you're not part of a criminal network. If you only heal people where are your victims? Yet to serve a non-addictive, nontoxic, healing tea from your garden is a crime! This is not based on any study, statistics, or research - it's just associated to the "War on Drugs," that some yank president declared years ago - a law that has been a monumental failure. There are thousands of years of anecdotal knowledge that these medicines are beneficial and transformative - yet it's criminal to make it into a healing tea or extract its magic essence.

Personally, I'm thankful I've never been to the Amazon nor met a Shaman. I don't have any linage or cultural context. I can proudly say, I've been totally trained by my vine. It's called a "teacher plant," so I let it teach me. This new fusion of Ayahuasca, is the best of the Amazon and the best of Australia and this combination wants no parameters or cultural restraints on what it can show humanity. Of course, I always pay respect to and acknowledge both cultures and use their music and art as vital tools.

In the Amazon, they have been conducting Ceremony for a couple of thousand years but there is no better place in the world to do Ceremony than Australia. 50,000 years of ceremonial culture and very present ancestral Spirits. I always acknowledge the traditional owners of the land and invite those spirits into my medicine and my space. I hop on the coat tails of that great energetic imprint. The plants will let you know if you're serving in the right or wrong way. Your ceremony will be chaos if not in accord with the "plant agency," that intercedes with these things. We are all under the same "auditing," these things have a self-regulating factor.

My direct elder is John Seed the great Australian Deep Ecologist, and whilst I am his healer, he is still my Mentor. His demeanour and wisdom, inspire me to effect people like his work does.

Regarding the mainstreaming of Plant medicines, I had resistance at first but am slowly becoming more tolerant. These plant agents are so beneficial that they will still help people, even when being served by people with no foundations in the space. This is Spirit work - earth, body, and spirit business. Medical science only focuses on the body and mind. They are missing a crucial component. This is also what's missing from the mainstream dialogue. Spirit business.

To be constantly addressing the physical is pushing shit uphill. Spirit is incorrupt - perfect. Spirit cannot get cancer of PTSD or depression etc. When people die, they are quickly going to realise that they wasted their incarnation, focusing on anxiety and depression. We are a perfect spark of divine awareness. The medicine gives people a personal mystical experience. It dissolves the filters of our Spirit contract - the 'soul amnesia' that is placed on us from birth. When people have a tangible experience of Spirit, they can recalibrate their life. The body and mind can be observed, stuck in their ruminating groove. This is the major way I work, and what is totally missing from the mainstream dialogue.

Surely common sense must prevail and nature be decriminalised. What made the government think they could legislate against plants anyhow? That is playing God and effectively declaring extinction on a species. The main attribute of the underground has been the protection of species, genetics, and propagation. Indeed, our community has saved some rare and micro endemic species, and more are now being home cultivated than are growing in the wild. The staunchest underground dudes I know, don't facilitate, they just collect and protect rare plants.

The traditional Amazonian admixture plant; Psychotria Viridis (Chacruna) is a shrub that grows in the shadowy rainforest undergrowth. The Acacia grows in the full Sun, absorbing all the light codes. Throughout history the Acacia has always been the "Tree of Knowledge." From the Egyptians, Sufis to the Alchemists of the Western Tradition, and the Australian Aboriginals who had multiple uses for Acacia including initiation and sorcery. It is our legacy to establish good protocols for its use. Respect for its power and abilities. Historically it has always been the secret of the Priests, Alchemists and Shamans, but now with the rise of the internet - the genie is out of the bottle. We can expect to see a host of loungeroom shamans.

This book is a great way for Australian facilitators to share their knowledge and to ensure the formative voice of the Australian Underground is heard, recorded, and not lost. I think our Ceremonial work has gotten off on the right foot, there have been minimal deaths, injuries, and casualties. I'd like to see our benchmark for best practice on a continuous improvement curve.

CHAPTER TWO

Skye Cielita Flor - Ayahuasca

I grew up in South Africa, a country I adore for many reasons but also the murder and rape capital of world. My family are wonderful, deeply caring people and my childhood was full of love and joy, but my parents (particularly my father) are also very nihilist, rationalist, atheist, and materialist in their beliefs about the world.

Some of the unspoken core assumptions were essentially that life is about hard work and taking care of your family, that there is no essential meaning to any of it - if you can't see it or measure it then it doesn't exist - you try to have some fun where you can before something unfortunate happens and you die. From there it's just lights out and you get eaten by worms. All of it random, a kind of lucky mistake, or unlucky depending on the kind of life you are born into.

Dad believes that religion and spirituality are for weak people who can't handle the harsh and painful truths of existence. There was also a subtle kind of intellectual imperialism in my home, the belief that the further you stray from the rational the less intelligent you must be. As a result, I developed an intense fear of death and non-existence in my early teens. This was sparked off by my grandmother's slow and difficult death from cancer when I was twelve - followed by the sudden death of my beloved cat, two years later.

Add to this, the intensifying atmosphere of violence in South Africa and my fear grew into a monster of panic attacks, and anxiety. This combination of personal loss against a backdrop of hatred, violence, stark inequality, without any framework to make sense of it all, sent me into a deep existential crisis. No one knew quite what to do with me, and my uncomfortable emotions, as we certainly didn't have space to express them at home.

My panic attacks sent my heart to pounding, my palms sweating and I would feel tingles going up my left arm. This led to a trip to the doctors' rooms where I was monitored via EEG. All was deemed fine with my heart (physically at least), so it was clearly psychosomatic according to the doctor. But there was great stigma around getting any type of therapy so it was all swept under the rug.

Thankfully, I was a natural and irrepressible spiritual seeker from a young age and held a deep longing for something more alive and meaningful then the basically rationalist, materialist and atheist worldview I was given. My intuition was that this worldview wasn't true but I couldn't find anyone to mirror what, in my heart, I already knew. Christianity did not resonate with me at all. I lived on a farm with lots of animals and felt a deep and natural kinship with the non-humans. My mom was an herbalist and co-owned an apothecary and these two areas of life felt the most alive and mysterious - small cracks in the concrete floor of modernity - a place where the light got in.

Another light in the dark was encountering a person at school who went on to become one of my enduring best friends. He is a few years older than me and was brimming with a different kind seeing - the kind

I was hungry for. Finally, a human who was asking similar questions and a little further down the path! I still tingle with gratitude for this encounter and for all the ways it has shaped my life since.

He was very adventurous and after leaving school, ended up backpacking through India. Through a chance encounter with another backpacker, he heard about ayahuasca and ended up attending a retreat in the Peruvian Amazon in 2004. When he returned and told me all about it, it strongly sparked my curiosity. He encouraged me to go and experience the medicine for myself and I did so the following year. Ironically, I went to jungle on the small inheritance my grandma left me, basically enough to buy a plane ticket and entry into the retreat.

So, at 16, on my gap year (I was two years ahead at school), full of hope and anxiety, I attended my first ayahuasca retreat in the Peruvian Amazon. I sat in three ceremonies with a traditionally trained curandero and it totally changed my life. My anxiety and panic pretty much vanished after my first ceremony. This involved hours of repetitive visionary enactments of my death and decomposition in wild and gruesome ways. I cried out for someone to make it stop. I intensely grieved my own unlived life and resisted again and again. I prayed for mercy, begged for it to end and then I finally SURRENDERED.

I surrendered into a direct encounter with the Great Ocean of Being, the mysterious ineffable intelligence that cannot help but spontaneously and unceasingly spawn this existence. I spent what felt like a timeless eternity in a place beyond any self-identity or reference to "the human." There was a deep and clear transmission that everything is okay, even when it's not.

There was a vast awareness permeated by what I can only call love, although all words pale in the face of what this was. When my human mind started to reform itself towards the end of the ceremony, I recall laughing wildly at the worldview I'd been given. It was so painfully cramped, dead and exceptionally untrue. This existence is alive and absolutely brimming with intelligence, from the smallest microcosm to the largest macrocosm. It was so obvious as to be laughable. I have never been able to unsee what I saw that day, even when materialist thought patterns reassert, there is no doubt that my ground is alive.

Following this retreat, I travelled and worked around Europe for a year. I drank Ayahuasca in Glastonbury with some New Age hippies but it just wasn't the same. At the instruction of the plants, I returned to South Africa and spent three years studying traditional Chinese medicine in an apprenticeship. This was a brilliant foundation in understanding body and energy dynamics and perceiving patterns of health and imbalance. During this time, I drank ayahuasca with some visiting Brazilian healers, which was powerful, but still not what I was looking for. I then worked as a wilderness guide in the South African bush for a year, which was also profound. But again, the jungle kept calling and eventually I had to listen.

I finally returned to Peru in 2011, six years after my initial retreat and entered into five years full-time study in the jungle with indigenous Shipibo curanderos. I was very driven to find my teachers and commit to a traditional apprenticeship. I knew it was something I needed to do. I felt a deep love, connection, and fear for the medicine all at once. It felt like this was the medicine I needed for my own particular brand of Western neurosis - the medicine I needed to come back to life. I also knew I wanted to offer this to my community back home one day.

My original intention was to study and then return home to South Africa and open a healing centre or clinic that would offer a combination of Shipibo curanderismo and traditional Chinese medicine. I wanted to bring the plants to my community, alongside my two best friends who were studying with me - but life went in another direction and now I'm here in Australia and my friends are both in Europe. A large chunk of my community and family found a way to escape South Africa - which is a sad story for another time.

My apprenticeship was in holding ayahusca ceremony as part of a much wider system of traditional jungle medicine including master plant dietas, the art of diagnosis and formulating specific treatment protocols with a wide array of plant medicine preparations and other forms of energetic or animistic healing modalities. All are held within a deeply relational/animist framework or worldview. I also spent three months in the Sacred Valley, Peru, doing a 300-hour Shamanic Yoga Teacher Training, practicing Despacho and going on weekly, silent San Pedro cactus hikes with some Q'ero healers. I have also worked with Psilocybin mushrooms outside of a traditional framework since my teens and consider them dear friends and allies.

So, it's now nineteen years since my first ayahuasca ceremony. My full-time apprenticeship began thirteen years ago when I was twenty-three. I was twenty-eight when I left the jungle, so I've been working with these medicines in one form or another ever since - nineteen years of personal practise and thirteen years as a student and practicing facilitator.

While studying, I worked as a facilitator for the Ayahuasca Foundation in Peru (2011-2016) and assisted my teachers on their retreats. So basically, I spent five years running retreats for groups of ten people at a time, each retreat lasting between two and ten weeks. I was drinking ayahuasca every second night alongside my teachers.

After leaving the jungle I spent nine months running group retreats in South Africa alongside other experienced facilitators. I also worked one-on-one with folks but with a minimum of three ceremonies (Ayahuasca, Psilocybin and San Pedro cactus). Each ceremony was at least a week apart, sometimes two.

When I came to Australia in 2017, I decided to stop offering medicine to people. I was a guest facilitator on other people's retreats in New Zealand, India and South Africa. I wanted to focus on the practice of plant dieta, deep listening and integration. My focus has been on developing relationships with the land, plants, and spirits through the process of plant dieta, and my relationship with ancestral herbal medicines.

I've recently entered an apprenticeship in Deep Ecology with legendary Australian Rainforest Activist, John Seed. I also do Grief Ritual Training with Francis Weller, and Somatic Mythology training with Josh Schrei. My partner and I run workshops incorporating these frameworks and modalities. We feel that each of these is helping us to craft a contemporary Living Earth Framework and delivery system that brings the core teachings and transmissions from the plants into our actual day to day lives.

We've been invited to teach aspects of this work to Psychedelic Psychotherapy students. It feels vital to embed psychedelic work into living earth frameworks of this kind. I'm about to launch some workshop and study groups on building relationships with plants and partnering with plant spirits via the imaginal and dreaming realms. This is inspired by my plant dieta practice, which is really the core of the Shipibo curanderismo tradition - more so than ayahuasca ceremony I would say.

I may or may not return to psychedelic facilitation here in Australia, it feels like a big responsibility and quite risky in this cultural and legal context. As a new mother, I'm not sure I would want to take that chance. Once I've stopped breastfeeding, I'll take groups of people to visit our teachers in the jungle yearly or bi yearly. I also support people who need assistance in preparing for or integrating their plant medicine experiences.

So, while I'm not actively facilitating psychedelic work at present, my previous groups have been at dedicated retreat centres with my teachers in the jungle or in other parts of the world. My upcoming plant connection workshops and classes will be held in beautiful nature spots near my home and on the land, I live on.

When working with clients it's important to discuss clear boundaries. For example, it's not okay to have sexual relations of any kind with a participant. If a genuine interest in relationship develops, I would definitely recommend a cooling off period of at least a year before trying to follow that up and maybe some therapy to make sure it's a safe and sane thing to do.

Discussion around not pedestaling the facilitator or projecting sexual or saviour fantasies onto them is important and a clear understanding of the facilitators' role and where their responsibilities start and end. Clear communication about what behaviour is expected from them and what they can expect from me. It's important for clients to be honest in all screening questions and interviews.

There are so many positive stories of client healing, both physical and emotional. People with incurable illnesses, cancer, asthma, Hashimoto's, gut issues, thyroid disease. Women who've been infertile, can find themselves pregnant shortly after returning home from a retreat. We also worked with a man who had suffered with Crohn's Disease for most of his life and though the medicine didn't "cure" him, he experienced many years symptom free for the first time. The symptoms eventually returned, but were milder and more manageable. We believe this was a result of his massive emotional catharsis in combination with a powerful purgative called Ojé, a resin from a Fig tree, used by the Shipibo to clear the digestive tract.

I could share hundreds of stories of profound shifts in mental health and general wellbeing and vitality. Reconnection to a sense of purpose and direction. Many folks returning home to mend decade long family conflicts, resolving or dissolving of relationships and so much more.

In the Shipibo tradition, Ayahuasca is seen to be a powerful diagnostic force and a kind of spiritual conductor but not a force for healing as much as other plant spirits. As students of this vast healing tradition, we spend a large amount of time in "Plant Dieta" - basically, spending weeks in silent isolation, cultivating direct relationship with specific plant spirits that will then come through our voices in Ayahuasca ceremony, via healing songs called Icaros, and enact their healing potency on our clients. So basically, in our tradition, the stronger a healers dietas, the stronger the healing potency of their ceremonies will be. Dietas are also done to cultivate defences against forces we wouldn't want our clients encountering. In our tradition, you can't safely facilitate a ceremony without having undertaken many dietas.

So yes, there are miracle stories where medicine work leads to spontaneous remissions but I'm reluctant to place all the emphasis on these stories as it just sets up unrealistic expectations. The first two days of my retreats were often spent trying to break down people's expectations. People should know that in most cases the hard work comes AFTER the ceremony and that crisis often precedes this healing. So many folks want healing without the crisis that Aya often takes one directly into, both during and after ceremony.

In almost every retreat, I've had people lie to me about their conditions. Some failing to mention that they were suicidal and that ayahuasca was their last resort, which doesn't necessarily rule them out, but requires a more thorough delving into their mental stability and support networks back home and on the retreat. Some folks require specialist support that we just aren't qualified to give and it requires folks being honest for us to know where that line is.

Ayahuasca has the potential to seriously destabilize folks for a period afterwards. This can lead to profound breakthroughs with the right support but can also cause worsening if that support isn't available. Schizophrenics have had mental health breaks on retreats at the centre we worked for, as they failed to mention their condition. It's hard when folks are desperate and fearful about being turned away if they're honest, but it's important to know that not all places and spaces are equipped to deal with that. Our Peruvian teacher has successfully treated schizophrenia caused by ancestral spirit possession on multiple occasions, but never with Ayahuasca and over very long timelines.

For me, the most interesting part of this work is that, in the right environment, it can elicit an Eco-Awakening to the livingness or animism of the world. Western society has a pernicious misunderstanding of who we are in relation to life itself. This needs the right language, cosmology, rituals, and practices but this is the core wound of western humanity in my opinion.

Earth as a planet and everything in it; rocks, mountains, rivers, animals and of course the trees and plants are sentient and intelligent beings. Ayahuasca is considered a bridge towards the animacy of the jungle.

Ayahuasca opens your eyes to their spirit - their beingness. The healing comes from the relationship you have with the other but the container really matters. I absolutely know that people drinking ayahuasca in Australia don't get this full experience and that's not so much about where, it's about who and the context they carry with them.

Unfortunately, the Australian underground scene is rife with unwell people. Folks serving medicine after only a handful of ceremonies, or serving to prop up their own self-image, or for monetary reasons etc. But there are also some very wise and experienced underground facilitators who are self-taught and have been doing this for decades. It's a bit hard to navigate, especially if you don't know what to look for. Inexperienced clients have little clue how to sort the wheat from the chaff.

Many underground facilitators are making very strong brews and serving it to large groups of 20-40 plus people at a time. Typically, participants will drive a few hours into the countryside on a weekend, and blow their cranium out drinking Ayahuasca or an Ayahuasca analogue. (A brew containing MAOI and DMT plants not traditionally considered proper Ayahuasca, which is specifically Ayahuasca Vine and Chacruna or Chaliponga.) They then return to work within a day or two. For us, two weeks was the minimum retreat length and even that felt too short. Our groups were capped at 10 participants and we had multiple facilitators and assistants. There is such a deep cultural need for a "quick fix" and we saw that mentality infect the work with the plants a lot!

In my limited experience, I've seen the typical medicine scene here be dominated by a conspiratorial, new age framework. I haven't drunk (and probably wouldn't) with any underground practitioner in Australia. But my partner and I have heard many stories from folks who have felt damaged or harmed by people they drank with here. There are lots of people serving with minimal experience, who don't know what they are doing and don't even know that they don't know. I feel sad when I hear these stories. It gives the medicine a bad name and dilutes its potency and potential. Of course, there are also those doing great work! But again, how do clients navigate this? Most are quite clueless and only find their way after trying to heal from a bad experience.

From what I hear, there are a few people doing really good work in Australia without traditional training and I do believe a diversity of approaches is necessary, so I can appreciate that. But I trained in a system that takes YEARS of working in ceremony alongside teachers and undergoing many dietas before stepping into the role of facilitator. Five years would be the minimum.

In our tradition, you are required to build strong partnerships with the spirits of other plants and learn to work alongside them in ceremony for the purposes of healing and protection via Icaros before even considering taking on this role. Not to mention all the practices and treatments we give outside of the ceremony and one's skill in making a diagnosis. It's an entire system of medicine of which the ceremony is only one part and not necessarily the main part. It's hard for me to say that none of this matters and that anyone can just do this work if they have the calling. I wouldn't go a to Chinese medicine practitioner or acupuncturist who hadn't trained in the skill. I don't see this as different. So, for this reason, I don't typically consider myself part of the Australian psychedelic underground, although I suppose I am in another way.

Essentially, I've undergone an extremely rigorous and extensive training, and yet it's not even recognised by the above-ground here. There is a real grief in that for me. I wish it were different, but it isn't and so I adapt. I am applying the relational skills I learned within that context to build connections on this land, so that if I choose to work in that way again, my work will be empowered by strong relationships and be in direct connection with this land.

A lot of the underground folks make strong medicine on purpose. Acacia and Syrian Rue, (a combo commonly used by the underground here) is an Ayahuasca analogue, often super strong and a VERY different spirit to the ones we work with in the jungle. People are often disappointed with the strength of the medicine in the jungle, if they come from a background of using Syrian Rue analogues. The emphasis in the jungle is on sensitivity rather than strength. In fact, there are whole jungle traditions who work only with vine brews (MAOI) without Chacruna (DMT.) It's the vine that contains the deep wisdom. Chacruna is said to contain the light (visions) to illuminate the wisdom. It isn't necessary at all if you are sensitive and tuned in.

Only vine containing medicine should be called Ayahuasca. If it doesn't contain the vine, it's not Ayahuasca, it's a DMT Ayahuasca analogue. The spirit is different. In my tradition, the plants in the brew make a big difference to the experience. Firstly, there are different types of Ayahuasca Vine and each variety leads to a different kind of medicine. It is also known that old vine which you have a relationship with will make wiser, deeper medicine then a young vine that you don't have a relationship with. It matters.

In the jungle, a Cielo Ayahuasca Vine and Chacruna brew will be very different from a Black Ayahuasca Vine and Chaliponga brew. And a brew made from your beloved 50-year-old vine growing outside your house will be vastly different from the two-year-old vine you bought in a sack from a guy at the market. And whatever brew you drink will be different if it's guided by a curandero with 50 years of dietas vs.

a ceremony with an apprentice. I wish folks would use more precise language when talking about "the medicine" and ceremonies. Not all medicine or facilitators are equal, the range is vast.

Some jungle curanderos might add Toe (datura) to their brews to add extra visionary strength, as the tourists feel it's not working properly if they don't get a mind-blowing visual. It's the pressure of the market place to give people the experience that they paid for, which exerts pressure on indigenous healers and changes their way of working. My teachers always expressed that it's because westerners don't know how to listen, so they want the plants to scream in their faces. This feels true to me. I have personally experienced in myself and others, very deep work being done without any visionary content in the ceremony. It's truly not necessary for everyone.

The work, as I have learned how to do it, is all supernatural - it's relational and it's animist. Receiving an Icaro (song) is the experience of the spirit of the plant coming into your body through the song and channelling itself through you. You, as a facilitator are channelling the spirits - so it's all supernatural

Regarding initiation - the training is the initiation. It puts you through your paces. You are taking plant medicines that push you to the edge. You can be feeling like you're dying but are still forced to function and operate in ceremony - both looking after yourself, but still handling your business as a facilitator and supporting others. Sometimes the Curanderos will have to pick up the pieces if you cave in, which is okay because we always work in teams. Some of these initiations are spontaneous, while some are initiated by the teachers. The plants are tricksters – you are constantly tested by the plants on this path. How dedicated or committed are you? It's not a love and light path. You must have strength. You have to keep choosing the path over and over.

Ideally, people who are considering facilitating plant medicine should undergo traditional training. I'd only drink with someone who'd done many years of medicine work themselves and had experienced high macro-doses and navigated themselves through the ensuing crisis.

They need to be rooted in the land in a respectful way. They need to be emotionally, psychologically well, and aware of and responsible for their own shadow. They need to have a good idea of what ego aspects are driving them to this work - we all have those, even the old jungle curanderos in my experience. And while everyone needs to earn a living, this work should not be purely money motivated. Medicine work is one part of a whole system, an ecology, which takes years to hone. There are very few people I'd recommend in Australia.

Adding my two cents about some of the big shifts currently unfolding in the global psychedelic movement, particularly the legalisation of certain substances for use within psychedelic assisted therapy. I'll say off the bat, that I'm ultimately for full legalisation within all contexts and generally prefer an atmosphere of trusting adults to make their own decisions about what they do and don't ingest, for whatever reasons they choose.

A healthy ecology has diversity, and a diversity of approaches feels more necessary now than ever. However, that is not our reality at this moment. Instead, we are seeing only psychiatrists and the odd psychotherapist being given the green light to administer these medicines within the therapeutic context. Until very recently, these institutions have demonised and pathologized these medicines and the altered states they engender. Of course, there have always been exceptions - Stan Grof comes to mind - so it seems bizarre to me that they are now the legal gate keepers of these medicines.

Having a background as a traditionally trained Ayahuasca ceremonialist within the Shipibo tradition, part of me is quite ambivalent about this sudden enthusiasm around psychedelic plant medicines and the ways they are now being embraced by mainstream psychology. I'm speaking specifically to plant medicines, not MDMA, and Ketamine - which I think is fantastic.

Naturally, I'm celebrating the fact that suffering people will have an easier time accessing plant medicines that can provide genuine relief. I'm also enjoying the ways in which it seems to have softened the cultural judgement towards these medicines and provoked needed conversation around their use. But part of me is concerned that 'The Spectacle,' is attempting to co-opt, decontextualise, standardise and monetize a powerful rewilding force. You can argue that it was already happening within the psychedelic tourism movement to a lesser degree but the prioritisation of this one context over the others is another attempt to gain control over something powerful that it was starting to lose its grip on. Part of me also laments what will become an increased use of these medicines outside of the traditional containers.

And if I'm honest, I suppose I'm frustrated that folks with a psychotherapeutic background are being given the green light, while those of us with years of traditional training will still have to practise illegally and at great personal risk. Not to mention the fact that indigenous peoples, the keepers of these medicines and associated traditions, who have hundreds, if not thousands of years of history and unbroken lineages of practice and transmission will also fall under the banner of "illegal" practitioners. This doesn't make any sense.

I'm also perplexed by the number of people being certified to administer these medicines with little, to no direct experience themselves; as if being a psychiatrist or psychotherapist somehow automatically qualifies you to hold space for entheogenic medicine experiences. Being a therapist and ceremonial plant medicine facilitator are two different skillsets in my opinion, maybe complimentary, but not the same.

In fact, I think it's very wise for Westerners to have ongoing therapeutic support both before and after the ceremony - just like I'm totally on board with more traditionally trained and underground facilitators being trauma-informed. But to leave out the animistic, relational side of this work is a devastating fragmentation of something precious and a continuation of a dangerous trend of de-animation that is responsible for so much of the mayhem unfolding in the world today.

I sat in ceremony with my teachers in the jungle, every second night for years - years! I underwent, and continue to undergo, dozens of master plant dietas. I diligently apprenticed to the many different aspects of that tradition, a tradition in which ayahuasca ceremony is only a tiny part of a much larger, nuanced, and multifaceted system of healing. I am still considered a rank beginner by their standards. There are very good reasons for that, and if you have gone deeply enough into that world, then you understand why that is.

But all this is happening regardless of what I think about it, and I suppose I'm curious about where this will lead and its impact on the larger pattern. And that part that doesn't really know much about much, also wonders if this might be part of a larger, plant-based, earth-based agenda. Maybe I need to trust the plants a bit more, maybe it is they who are co-opting the industry and not the other way around?

Since it's happening anyway, I'd like to add my voice to what I'd like to see happening in this emerging field, because even though I'm a beginner that knows nothing from one point of view, I'm simultaneously someone with a great deal of experience from another, even if I don't talk about it openly very often. So firstly, I'd like to see the people who are being certified to administer plant medicines having direct macrodose experiences within different contexts. And ideally, some of those experiences should be with skilled practitioners from traditional shamanic/animist lineages, so they can be introduced to the roots of this work and hopefully gain an appreciation for these profound old-world ways of working.

Ideally, they will be encouraged to have challenging encounters with their own psyches on these medicines and given the opportunity to work through them with skilled support from both psychotherapeutic and Shamanic perspectives. Hopefully, this will foster a better understanding of the forces that their clients will meet and then come to see the value of the different approaches. I would like to see therapists having a direct experience of the limitations of their paradigm and be humble enough to call on traditionally trained shamanic practitioners if the situation is called for - and vice versa of course.

I'd like to see a strong focus on bringing awareness to and mapping the contours of the unconscious, unquestioned assumptions of our cultural story, because these experiences are always taking place within a context and that context matters and influences both the experience and the integration and sense-making of that experience. For most of us in the West, that will be the anthropocentric, hyper-individualist, reductive, rationalist, materialist, consumer focused, profit prioritising, desacralized, white, male-dominated culture of objectification and de-animation in a time of late-stage capitalism and ecological collapse.

Following on from that, it feels really important that other more life-affirming stories and meaning-making frameworks are identified and introduced in its place; Deep Ecology, Cosmogenesis, Systems Thinking, The Holistic Gaian Sciences, Taoism, Eco-Buddhism, Paganism and

Earth-Honouring Animistic Traditions. If you can't find a Relational Living Earth framework to embed these experiences within – then the Story of Separation will likely be the default soil in which these experiences take root. So much to say on this point in particular.

I'm of the opinion that engagement of plant medicines, in individual and group settings, centred within relational living earth cosmology is deep medicine for the very particular wounding of the Western psyche. This is an area of particular passion and interest to me; one I intend to write more about and I suspect it will be in this area that I serve the movement taking place. I want to see these medicines respectfully embedded, not extracted, as is our habit with everything we take a fancy to in the West.

So much more to say on every point I've already mentioned and so many more points I could mention, such as cultural appropriation, part of the profits derived from plant medicine work going back to indigenous wisdom keepers and protection of forest ecologies, taking medicines out of the office and onto the land, bioregionalism and so much more. But I think I'll leave it here for now. It always feels a bit edgy throwing my own words out into the world, so I'll just say that I totally reserve the right to have a different answer if you ask me about this again tomorrow.

CHAPTER THREE

Julian Palmer – Ayahuasca, Cactus, MDMA

I grew up in a pedestrian, friendly enough, calm part of the world - North East Victoria, Australia. My childhood was idyllic in some ways, but definitely far from perfect. I was troubled with mysterious illnesses as a child - such as having a very low, white blood cell count from 2 to 5 years old and I was on antibiotics during that time.

Growing up, the world as it was presented to me wasn't interesting to me at all, so I started to seek out the other worlds and endeavoured to have out of body experiences. Both my mother and grandfather had had such experiences. My grandfather was a prisoner of war in Burma and would go out of his body in the severe conditions of the concentration camp. My mother discovered that she could do same thing – usually in times of high stress. She could float above her body. She told me when I was older that in this state, she would try to teach me a yogic technique. This wasn't the normal way she would talk!

When I was 15, I tried to have such out of body experiences. I would meditate every night for an hour but I never managed to achieve it. However, I did have a kind of spiritual awakening. This manifested as a great deal of anxiety because I saw the truth of realities behind appearances. I could feel entities around me, which terrified me at the time. I started to go crazy and rebelled against everything.

I went to Wanganui secondary school in Shepperton, Victoria and ended up becoming vice captain of my school in year eleven, through a speech that made fun of everyone. Then I began critiquing my environment through artistic pranks. I received a lot of validation from my classmates for this, strangely enough and became quite popular. But I was very happy to leave school and I took a gap year and travelled to America and Europe.

I discovered LSD in Height Ashbury, San Fracisco when I was 18. I found more LSD in London, then again at a festival. My most memorable LSD trip was when I once took 400 micrograms while on a bus trip between San Francisco and Los Angeles. It took four years to process that trip and what I saw about humanity, the reality behind appearances.

I would say I started to wake up to a spiritual reality when I was sixteen. I found my wings being clipped as I perhaps got too close to the sun. I started to see too much and got attacked by entities. For example, I jumped off a moving train to see what would happen. I liken this to the devil whispering in my ear. The injury I received is only just now healing. I spent my late teenage years and early twenties trying to understand what those wings were and how to get them back. I was into eastern mysticism, 'Advaita' and was really trying to rediscover my spirit, which I felt I had lost. So, I really explored everything, including psychedelics from eighteen onwards.

In the 1990's, I considered the psychedelic scene to be very spiritually immature at the time, perhaps even more so than it is now. By that I mean, where was the serious ontological foundation and ethos in all of this. As in, why were we doing this? It seemed for most, more about cool experiences than spiritual exploration. But I was more inquisitive.

Being a full on psychonaut is not a long lifespan as there always comes a reckoning and that reckoning usually scares most people off and they give it up. Even now there's no clear and firm acknowledgement of another reality within the general psychedelic scene. There's a kind of throwaway psychonaut curiosity, not grounded in any serious comprehension of reality, or spiritual basis.

In late 1999, I found myself unemployed. I had been a web designer, until my boss decided to move to Iceland to marry an Icelandic woman. I realised at this time that psychedelics were to become my new job. It was obvious to me that psychedelics were a tool to engage with the truth of spiritual realties and so psychedelics became my full-time job from then until now.

I started actual medicine work in December 2001. I harvested a bunch of Acacia phyllodes and learnt how to prepare a psychoactive tea by combining them with Syrian Rue. I learned about this from some old UseNet posts from the mid-nineties. In January 2002, I took my tea to "Confest," a conference/festival in rural Victoria. It just seemed the natural order of things to share the Acacia tea with the people I met there, since I was there giving talks on psychedelics.

So, I gave the people my tea, a mix of Syrian Rue and Acacia Phlebophylla. It was completely magical and otherworldly. Everyone who took it was changed in a pretty profound way, so this encouraged me to want to continue to share this medicine with people in this way.

The medicines I mainly work with, are the various high DMT containing Acacias mixed with Ayahuasca (Caapi vine) or sometimes with Syrian

Rue. I work with these medicines primarily because I have discovered that the different varieties of DMT acacia have unique voices and quite different messages for the people who drink them.

I also brought the concept of cactus walks from South Africa to Australia in 2013. In South Africa there are groups who do this every week and there is quite a strong culture of people growing cactus and preparing it themselves. I find this medium to be brilliant as it creates a lot of optimism, intersocial safety and connection to nature and ourselves. This works to really raise people out of any funk or stuck place or anxiety they may be experiencing.

The last few years I've been working with a weekend format where we go on a cactus walk on the Saturday, then take MDMA together on the Sunday. I've found this format works very well for people, to experience a felt sense of connection with other people, and become less defended and more aware of who they are, how they are being and how they CAN be, and how LIFE can be. "Best Weekend Ever," is very common feedback from these weekends.

I first started guiding people with psychedelics and giving DMT to hundreds of people starting in early 2000. DMT was such a fascinating medium, and me and my friends at the time found it exciting, trying to understand this phenomenon which was not well known at all at the time.

One time I took 28 people on top of Bald Rock near Tenterfield for Exodus festival in 2003 and gave them an acacia brew. There were a lot of the key people from the psychedelic world there at that time. A couple even got married from meeting at that group. The feeling of interconnection, and the vibe created a kind of interconnected convergence of true happening. I've often found that to be quite addictive, like a little party which was truly happening and enlivening.

Overall, the positives of this work just kind of blend together, with this feeling of liberation and joy that comes from being able to catalyse big shifts in people's lives – it's given me a great sense of fulfilment. Seeing people's lives shift is always a big positive. Some people might have instantaneous awakenings and go from being atheists to believers or they might go from being miserable to experiencing happiness after just one experience. But it is even more interesting to watch people slowly change over time, letting go of their deep troubles and trauma, and moving forward with their life in a much more positive way.

But it's not all sunshine and roses - in fact things can definitely go south. I once had a guy go completely crazy. He started trying to attack the other participants, and was even trying to gouge out people's eyes. I had to fight him off them. He was possessed like a crazy animal, scratching and biting. I was left bloody and still have scars to this day. We had to search for his two front teeth which we found under a pillow the next day. But he had a huge healing and his life changed forever. He stopped taking drugs every night and partying and settled down with a good woman - but it took me six months to recover from that night.

In regards to the mainstreaming of plant medicines there just doesn't seem to be much, if any, awareness about so many potential issues. Theres a kind of blind arrogance and a lack of listening to, not just the underground, but also indigenous peoples. Scientism seems to rule the technocratic, materialistic viewpoint, but science will not help people to understand this vast "game" of life which psychedelics amplify, its terrain and characteristics and how it really works. You can only understand that by actually taking the plants and immersing yourself deeply in these spaces. These spaces are very strange and wondrous, very mind expanding and way, way, way beyond the limited scopes and understandings of science.

What is also missing from the mainstream dialogue on plant medicines is that there seems to be a lack of understanding that these substances connect people to the numinous, to the spiritual nature of the universe. What we're seeing, is an ideological rift that science has between the religious and therefore the spiritual. But perhaps it is time that science begins to measure and understand the metaphysical dimensions. Psychedelics are most likely going to be a catalyst to that project.

The basis of my work is allowing people to engage with the spirit of the plants. Allowing people that dialogue is fundamental to this work occurring. The whole point of this work is to create a space for the miracle of healing to occur in relationship to the plants.

It's my observation, that most plant medicine facilitators will experience some kind of an initiation. Mine occurred between March 2000 and March 2002. At this time, I was probably taking psychedelics two or three times a week. I was involved in a deep process of understanding and inquiry, a deeper work which unfolded with the elements of this earth and its potential evolution.

I'd meet hundreds of entities, and felt I was doing an extremely potent work on behalf of the collective consciousness. I was witnessing an evolutionary process, for example, architects showing me new prototypes of human technology. All this work was enmeshed in an understanding of a whole new human operating system - communicating via telepathy for example, a new template of human language, creating a whole new game.

Something in me wanted a liberation. I had this transcendental fire, passion and drive. I probably presented as completely crazy to others. Others around me at that time were more into Hedonism. But I saw that this was my job now. It was a full-time job. I was actually on the brink of insanity and was practically homeless. I was staying with friends, camping on the beach, getting temporary accommodation when I could. During this two-year initiation period, I purged out every intensity and seeking.

It changed in 2002 when I met a woman who was even more experienced with psychedelics than me. She validated me and the work I was doing. We engaged on these levels and I was somehow free to move forward after that. I became sane, my mind stabilised. This process was deemed complete when I had an experience of marrying a cyberpunk priestess in the heart of infinity. I was so driven and then after meeting that woman, I got more settled and got a girlfriend. Two years after that, Changa was born. Changa is a DMT smoking blend that I created, which, when done correctly, provides a 10-20-minute sub-breakthrough DMT experience.

My advice to anyone considering facilitating plant medicine and what they most need to know, is that this work is an extension of where they are at in their own inner life, work and healing. Whatever is going on inside of you is going to be amplified and tested many times over doing this work. You cannot really do this work properly if you are too self-involved or narcissistic. You need to be free enough of your own patterns and "shit" to be present to another person and give up your own egocentric stories and not play silly power trips or games of the world. You really do need to have freed yourself from many of the accoutrements of the mind and the ego. Psychedelics give you an opportunity to be able to be in this still space, and not give the egotism of the world any credence or credibility. This type of self-work can take many years.

People who are considering consuming medicine need to know that our society doesn't really understand the seriousness of these altered states. They think that their mortgage and job is far more important! The state of your soul matters so much more than your survival. In a country like Australia, people don't really understand spiritual realities, whereas in a country like Brazil, there is greater awareness of such things. Psychedelics will bring people an awareness of spiritual realities, beyond the desiccated and shallow world view of technocratic consumerism.

There is not just the wondrous and the sublime, there is the horrifying and the terrifying. We need to develop new kinds of muscles that our atrophied society has not prepared us to face - the intensity of the spiritual warfare we might encounter. You need to get really humble, really fast, if you want to grow and you've got to see where you might not be up to the task AT ALL! But giving up and lying in a ditch, and taking the blue pill of illusory oblivion is simply not an option.

Over time you learn how to play the game of life in its most essential form, that at first looks completely overwhelming, and in that process, you might fall off your horse again and again. There is no space for fear in this work. If you experience a fear of something, you need to stop and address it - confront it full on, before moving forward. That might take months. But fear can wipe you out completely. Stress and fear are the biggest enemy of the human body and soul. It will age you and corrode your ability to be present to reality.

As far as I can see, the underground is where the real work is occurring. The overground may do some good treating people's issues like PTSD.

But ultimately, everyday people are seeking a real spiritual connection, they are wanting to come into a true connection with themselves and other people. They want to be happy; they want to be free of suffering and they want an optimal life as well.

Maybe in a decade or two the overground will catch up with the underground. At the moment, it seems to me like the overground is implicitly pushing this view that society is somehow ok, and then just appearing to fix people, and send them back to the world – when in fact, the world we have created, is very often toxic to the mental health of people.

In my view, trauma has its origins in entities and entity possession. I don't see the trauma as arising from the individual, but from the attacks that have their origin in entities. Alcohol for example – there's a reason it's called spirits. When someone is drunk, they open themselves up to entities. Indigenous people typically have massive issues with alcohol. Entities can take over your body to a strong degree and are waiting in the wings for that opportunity. Sexual abuse and domestic violence usually occur under the influences of alcohol. Although this is very prevalent, it's hardly ever talked about.

In the cases of shock and trauma, entities can also attach. This is also missing in the debate. Some people reckon they are "trauma informed" but many don't comprehend the elements pushing them. Of course, there are also sociological elements, particularly the conflation of sex and love. Malevolent energies gain a lot of food from human sexuality.

Probably the overground is going to go through a lot of weird, heavy and crazy stories to realise this. Even with MDMA, I've seen people go into demonically possessed states, and I don't think the overground is in any way prepared to deal with these kinds of states in any respectful or meaningful way which creates liberation and healing.

But I don't think the overground is doomed, I think there are some good cookies in the overground, as well as some absolute scum. It is the lack of humility that concerns me and the adherence to these limited mental forms and understandings of our spiritually unenlightened time, which don't at all reflect actuality. I do think what we're seeing often, is a real lack of ontological open mindedness and theological flexibility, which, if you are really taking psychedelics, are qualities you have to develop. The issue is, a lot of people are not seriously taking, say the tryptamines, in high enough doses regularly and don't have a serious practice.

Perhaps many people will eventually make the case that we need to put psychedelics back in the box, because we don't know how to fully appreciate and deal with their power, but psychedelics are only tools which are showing us the truth of reality beyond the limited mental conceptions and that truth is strange, people are resistant to seeing it for many reasons.

Much change is coming for the human race. People are deceived by their minds and egos - fear of what others think. They are susceptible to shiny solutions. In western society, evil can influence us by presenting an option that looks good. But the road to hell is paved with good intentions. Many people are sitting ducks. For example, birds won't typically eat genetically modified food. Many people don't trust their gut or are really in tune with it. They are told something is good for them, even if it makes them feel unwell. They continue taking it, be it prescription drugs, vaccines, genetically modified food, chlorinated and fluoridated water.

Make your choices very carefully, because you could end up on the weaker team which ends up in the ditch. Most people are obscured in making the right choices by their enmeshment in limited mental forms and their egoic forms. The whole purpose of psychedelics, if you ask me, is really to get out of your ego and your mind, and come back to your heart, your gut, your truth. Stay on target. Your gut knows the truth, your heart knows the truth.

CHAPTER FOUR

Juliana Wright – Iboga

My father was in the RAF so I pretty much grew up on Airforce bases. What I mainly remember about that, was that timing was very important – I had to be on time. My mum had polio. I really loved my darling mama and had a real empathetic rapport with her. I was an only child and very independent. I spent my life with horses in the countryside – other people's horses, not my own. Later I went to Oxford University and got a fine arts degree - then painted portraits. I met my husband and we had two babies, so I spent twenty years bringing up children, on my own, as my husband and I split up.

I was always seeking. I had a drive, a desire – I didn't know what it was but I was always searching for something. I was strongly involved in the 5-Rhythms dance movement which was great for both embodiment practices and meeting likeminded people.

In my mid-forties I ran ceremonial magic groups for five years. This involved ritual and ceremony and the theme of invoking ancient archetypes, like Lilith; a figure in Mesopotamian and Jewish mythology, theorized to be the first wife of Adam. Lilith was the primordial she-demon, a feral, wild woman, who was eventually banished from the garden of Eden for disobeying Adam. Lilith refused to be dominated by men. Eve was her opposite; the archetypal domesticated woman who submitted to men's domination. Woman should never submit to men as they are equal. Anyway, it was a successful and very enjoyable endeavour and it was here that I first learned about the importance of ritual and ceremony.

Plant medicine found me - I wasn't looking for it. My introduction into the world of plant medicine happened after a random invitation to an ayahuasca ceremony. My good friend said to me; 'You have to come to this ayahuasca ceremony.' It was held at the village hall on Dartmoor, England, in the early spring of 2010. There were twenty people there and it was run by an efficient man who really knew his stuff. This triggered a two-year intensive of participating in fortnightly medicine ceremonies where I was introduced to all the main medicines: Ayahuasca, San Pedro, Kambo and Iboga. I was 66 when I started - I'm 77 now.

For the first nine months I really explored ayahuasca. One or two of the ceremonies I attended are memorable for their colour, intensity, entertainment, and shamanistic integrity. Mostly they were memorable for the noise and nonsense that the self-professed shamans created. However, and this is important I sense, the medicine went to work on me despite all these unnecessary distractions. That may have been because of my state of being at the time of my introduction to these medicines. My state of being at this time was due in large part to the wisdom and teachings of Barry Long.

A good friend had introduced me to the teachings of Barry Long; an Australian spiritual master who emerged on the world stage in the 1980s, with his ground breaking teaching on love, sex, truth, relationship, enlightenment and being in the present. He was the first Western spiritual teacher asking people to get into their bodies back in the '60's. (Unheard of at that time.)

He observed often in his teaching sessions, that people are not ready to give up their unhappiness unless they have suffered enough. This is true. Since 2010, I've been free of unhappiness and live in paradise, thanks to Barry Long's practical teachings and my epiphany on Iboga. I work mainly with people who have 'suffered enough' and want to change their reality and take responsibility for their unhappiness. The Wood (Iboga) helps them to get clarity on this.

One of Longs main themes is about getting your life right. I had achieved a state of non-thinking, meaning that I was living largely in the present moment and in my body. So, when life presented me with my plant medicine experiences, and I encountered the various intelligences, I needed and wanted nothing from them. I just surrendered.

Ayahuasca wiped the floor with me. I purged for all the world. At the time it felt ok and the purification on all levels was quite noticeable. I have to say that most of my ayahuasca experiences were difficult. I was really struggling. The quality of the medicine was pretty bad and I ended up purging all of the other participant's crap. On a positive note, my being was more purified as a result. After that, I decided to start drinking ayahuasca on my own. That helped me to become ego free and a better facilitator.

One very powerful experience I had, was when I was contacted by a very high vibrational archetype. The medicine had raised my vibration so that I went up to meet it as a carcass on a hook. My own consciousness was still present in this carcass. It had lowered its own vibration to meet me. I felt such a huge bestowal of grace from it and a great debt of gratitude.

Another profound experience I had, was doing an Ayahuasca ceremony with Darpan in a Rajasthani wedding tent outside of Glastonbury.

There were eighty people there. His medicine is superb. It was there that I asked ayahuasca to prepare me to meet the consciousness of Iboga. She did a phenomenal job on me. Even now I am in awe of what that medicine did to enable me to surrender to Iboga. San Pedro was phenomenal as well.

My intensive with the medicines ended in 2012. I had an epiphany and also knew that I wanted to offer iboga. My epiphany on the Wood was profound. The Wood is a real initiation - your reality changes. It grounded my experience of truth and showed me that love is the medium for truth. This place of truth is very cold, clear, and empty. The Amanita mushroom lords showed me the place of truth and invited me to enter this place - but I couldn't do it. It was too terrifying. I just wasn't ready for it. It was too cold, too clear - so I came back into existence, to the place of love. The place of truth is very profound.

My life has been a series of initiations as has my medicine work and my ceremonial magic. Iboga was definitely an initiation, as was ayahuasca - a huge grief purge. Meeting Lucifer was interesting, first in one of my solo rituals during my Western ceremonial magic period, as a vast resplendent, masculine energy being, incandescent with cold white light. It wanted to make me its creature but I wasn't impressed. My perception was that at some level, this exalted being was in immense pain. To me the pain (maybe it was a projection) always has a flavour. I saw in him, the grief of time immemorial. I said to him that I refused to be seduced and basically told him to fuck off.

Alistair Crowley also used to come into my ceremony space and I told him to fuck off as well, he was just there lurking in my space. When you hold these spaces, you are opening yourself up to curiosity from many beings. I was very clear. I feel I have been doing this ceremonial work for a long time in previous past lifetimes.

I also met Lucifer in real life. I was working as a mortgage advisor in 2000. This guy befriended me. He thought I was some important person. He told me that the world was mine to command. I said I wasn't interested in commanding the world. I asked if he was Lucifer. He said that, 'yes he was.' Barry Long talks about meeting Lucifer in his biography. I feel that my resonance or vibration is now in the same psychic field as Barry Longs. He died in 2003. Everything I have experienced on the medicine is a validation of everything he teaches. The medicines gave me a direct experience, not a concept, about love, truth, God, and life.

At the end of my ayahuasca intensive, Iboga arrived on the scene. I had the same expectations of it as my ayahuasca experiences - but it was very different. I didn't purge at all and just experienced the bliss and nothingness deep in my body during that ceremony. Upon surfacing and integrating during the following hours, I experienced an epiphany. Iboga had taken me out of the mirror of existence. I was no longer magnetised to the world but magnetised to source. In the world, but not of it. This was and is my magnetic shift.

It was from this place that my ceremonial offering was born. Primed by the five-year, ceremonial magic group, I'd facilitated back in the early nineties. I know how to hold the crucible of a ceremonial space and administer a sacrament and allow what follows to have the space to materialise. So, from my own experiences comes the ground of what I offer: mainly the importance of surrender and the trap of expectations.

So, my whole life has bought me to this moment where I'm offering medicine. The way I offer it and the wisdom I have, to share with people is from a clear and conscious space. I conduct small intimate gatherings in my own home, with only two people at a time. There is a mandatory, two months minimum, preparation period during which time, I introduce people to much of what I have learnt from Barry Long's teachings – mainly about stopping thinking, getting into the body, particularly the solar plexus, facing the inner demons and emotions by entering the body. Microdosing iboga is a great ally in this sometimes-daunting endeavour.

After my first Iboga ceremony I saw that I could offer people a much better experience than I had experienced. The ceremonies I attended were far too big – twenty people or more. One was even eighty people. The food was awful and I just found it difficult to stay in my body and in my own space and my own stillness. Stillness is where everything arises. I decided to do it in my own home so I could cook lovely food. I live on a forty-foot house boat on The Thames in Twickenham.

I've served plant medicines for about eleven years now. The first six years, I served ayahuasca. People told me that the medicine I made was some of the best that they had ever drunk. But it also undid a lot of people. They came apart. I was doing these sessions on my boat back then and it was far too difficult in that small space. There was no room for any helpers.

I now just work with Iboga. I switched to Iboga in 2016. It's such an easy medicine to deal with. Iboga is a straight forward medicine to serve, unlike ayahusca, as people can't move around. On ayahuasca you get people moving around - men wanting to take their clothes off or get into bed with people. I have also offered San Pedro cactus and I used to serve Kambo but I don't anymore, except when people go into an Iboga ceremony with me. Kambo works well with Iboga as it is a mind interrupter. My Kambo stick is programmed to work with the wood.

Tabernanthe Iboga, affectionately called 'The Wood,' is a shrub from Equatorial Africa related to Jasmine, Gardenia, and Coffee. It takes seven years for the root bark to be ready for medicinal use. The older the Wood the stronger the actives. The best Wood I have had, was twenty years old. The bark is stripped without killing the shrub. It is then dried and shredded. The dose of dried Wood for ceremony varies between 10 to 30 grams. Even in small doses the Wood is a mind interrupter. It brings on stillness and beauty. In larger doses it induces ataxia. It really wants you to lie down, not move, and get into your body. My observation is that it acts on the electrical system in the body.

"Iboga is the godfather of all plants on the earth. There are many powerful plants out there that people use for visions and for healings. Every plant on the planet has healing properties. You just have to know them. Iboga is the chief plant, like the chief spirit. You have the spirits of the earth, the spirits of the sun, the spirits of the fire, the spirits of the water, and the spirits of the wind. Every element has a chief spirit. Iboga is the chief plant spirit. Iboga is the master, the godfather of all plants. Iboga understands all the plants on earth. ~Moughenda

According to the Bwiti, only the "anointed" or "consecrated" are gifted by the spirit of Iboga to offer an initiation or rite of passage, from one reality, or way of living, to another. The first thing I say to people who come to the Wood through me is, "Are you ready for your reality to be changed?" If you are, then your initiation starts here, in this moment of waking up to the realisation that there is more to your life than you thought. Iboga offers the potential for a 180 degree turn in living. From the thinking mind, the intellect, to the intuitional wisdom deep inside the body. As a root, Iboga gets to the root of the disconnection. It earths. It grounds you back into your body.

The whole world has lost the plot and operates from outside the body, in the head, in fantasy and ignorance. You can include yourself here. Iboga is going to change that, with a little help from me, help to begin the work necessary to lose your mind and go deep into the profundity of your body where the truth and beauty of what you really are is to be found. Then you can go out into the world as a living human being, an earthling. It's a coming home, to the love, stillness, the nothingness that you, in reality, are.

My preparation has an emphasis on introducing clients to Barry Longs teaching, because that's the route that took me to the medicine and the method that worked well for me and gave me my epiphany. The wood is all about truth and beauty. It took me into a place of truth. Everything fell into place. Even now while I talk about it, I get the feels. I see myself as being out of existence. My body is here but I am out of existence. Truth is a place out of existence. I am a watcher. We have chosen our body - a tool for the realisation of our divinity. Nature is my own sweet nature projected back for me to see.

People come to me through referral. I don't advertise. Nor do I have a schedule. I work organically. I have a private website. It includes all sorts of helpful suggestions. The preparation includes diet and a very strong emphasis on thought hygiene. Thinking causes all the problems in the world. People must get a handle on their thinking. Microdosing the wood is a good ally to help people see with more clarity and detachment from their nonsense – their thinking. They get to observe themselves.

I did an apprenticeship with a Bwiti trained, South African Shaman who was then living in Wales. I assisted him in ceremonies for two years. The Wood is now my mentor and ally. The Wood will be with you all your life. It's your greatest ally. It's true. Later, the Wood cleared it for me to offer ceremony together with my mentor, working with both medicines; ayahuasca and Iboga as well as Kambo. My mentor was then travelling the world doing ceremonies.

One thing that's not mentioned much in western circles, is the voodoo. I encountered this several times from Bwiti initiated Shamans. I find that misogyny is alive and kicking, and man's desire to control and manipulate my behaviour is shocking. One even paid a Tibetan monk to curse me because I refused to intervene in a problem he was having with my apprentice, who wasn't fitting in with his agenda. Recognizing and dealing with psychic attack is a vital skill when holding plant medicine rituals. I have the great good fortune of having learnt from Barry Long how to keep my space clear. So, curses do not get much purchase here! That chap is wasting his money and the monk's time.

Although I am based is in England, I am open to invitations from all over the world; including Australia, South Africa and Europe. I do bigger ceremonies in these places. It's hard work doing a big group - not just time consuming but also very energetically consuming, but I like the result. That's why I'm prepared to go through the hard work because I know the revelations at the end will be phenomenal.

My Australian connection started while I was running ceremonies in Malta. An Ozzie guy came and did some Iboga sessions with me then he invited me to come to Australia to do some ceremonies in Melbourne. That's where I first met Nick S, in 2016. I ran three ceremonies for sixteen people in total. Nick was one of them and he later said he wanted to assist me.

After an incident of my mentor's deportation, I stepped into the gap to serve in Australia. At that time there was no one offering the Wood in Oz. So, in January 2017, I started officially serving Iboga in Australia, Julian P, let me use his contacts which was very generous of him. He even did a little promo for me in one of his monthly newsletters, which I'm extremely grateful for.

I held another three Iboga ceremonies and saw sixteen people (two groups of six and one of four) in Sydney and Melbourne. The following year I went as well. I was all set to come back and had arrived in Sydney when the Covid lockdown started. I was also set to do Iboga ceremonies with therapists in South Africa, but the lockdown wiped that out as well. I was not going to get jabbed in order to travel.

I find Australians great to work with - they are very grounded, down to earth and no nonsense. In fact, the Australian influence is strong in my life with Barry Long of course but several others are mentioned as good guides to self-realisation in my preparation guidelines; Leila Jacobson and Darpan are included in there.

My assistant/guide Nick S, is a great addition to the team. He was also a memorable client. He'd been working extensively with ayahuasca prior to that. The Wood, as a potentiator, exposes people's nonsense, which can be a two-to-three-year unfolding. It really gave Nick a profoundly disturbing experience of what ayahuasca had stirred up in him. It exaggerated it. If you don't get the message, iboga will get the big stick out in ceremony. It will potentiate events until you get the message. Nick wrote an article on his Iboga experience for Medium. Here is a quote from it:

"Terrifying. Horrifying. Extreme torture. Tough love. Bitter medicine. 24 hours of hell realms within hell realms. Hilarious. These are some words that could be used to describe the juggernaut that was my New Years, Iboga Flood Dose experience."

"I thought I had been healing people, which no doubt I had been, but I had also been running away from all of my own problems, focusing on other people's healing processes in order to avoid having to deal with my own. Suddenly it was revealed to me that my Ayahuasca

use had really fallen off the wagon. This was not the responsible and respectable use of sacred entheogens for healing. Nay for me, it had degenerated into a type of codependency where I had been drinking so much medicine that it had been blinding me to the fact that I wasn't healing anymore, I was just spiritually bypassing under the guise of healing, getting lost in the fireworks of a brain full of serotonin and visions of otherworldly beauty that ultimately were escapist in nature and no longer related to reality anymore. Yes, it had started out as healing but by the end it was just more running away. The truth of this knocked the wind out of my guts and I just lay there shaking. How the fuck could this have happened? "You weren't grounded. You weren't careful. You weren't disciplined. You lost your way, Said Iboga." (Feb 2019, Nick S, Medium)

That's why preparation is so important and the Wood conveyed this to me. In my 40s, I did the beginning of Kabballah. My teacher had an acronym called 'The 5 P's' - patchy preparation gives piss poor performance. One must be 'prepared,' to go into an Iboga ceremony. What I bring to the preparation includes some of what I'd learned from Barry Long. His whole message was about living the truth, being true to the situation, the facts, not your feelings. When you look at the facts, the thinker and its attendant emotions are seen to be phonies. The Wood is intelligent and a great an ally in observing this. Once I can see the bullshit in myself, I can see the bullshit in the world (my mirror) and once I clear the mirror my reality changes.

The way I hold ceremony is very feminine - there is little control or rules. I trust the wood implicitly. People feel safe, they stay as long as they need. They usually arrive on Friday and leave on Sunday but can stay longer if they need another night. There have been many times where I have been in ceremony and had to leave while I was still in process. In saying that I do have some strict boundaries and have created a written agreement that clients must read and understand. I believe that the client is responsible for their own experience. I will provide a pristine space, but if they are not honest about their history, I won't take responsibility for the stuff they haven't told me. Working in a feminine way, means that I allow people to flow.

I'm always available to clients post ceremony but people rarely need me for that. The preparation is the key. I charge a non-refundable deposit so that people make a commitment to themselves. Two payments are made, one for the prep and one for the actual ceremony. They pay that a week before they come on the floor. If the medicine fails, by my interpretation, they will get some of their money back. Sometimes people don't come to the ceremony, they get cold feet.

People wanting to be facilitators and serve these medicines really need to be present, they need to be very grounded, and they definitely need to have taken lots of the Wood – this is a basic requirement. They need to come from their own experience, not some rhetoric. Rhetoric is so tedious. A lot of shamans do this - they latch onto something.

Another thing that facilitators need to deal with, is knowing how to handle people's projections. You need to know what a projection is and then how to deal with them. I've had curses put on me. I've been accused of being the antichrist and the devil. My response is clear; I'm just a mirror - my space is clear, I am empty. That is important. To be a true mirror, facilitators need to have done a great deal of personal work. They need a lot of life experience. I always speak from my own experience and people really feel that, they feel my grounded-ness, maturity, experience, and my truth.

Regarding my fears or challenges around serving the medicine, I occasionally find myself in self-doubt - fortunately I know how to dissolve it, but it can be pernicious and a distraction, particularly for women. I provide a pristine space, support, and encouragement. The medicine does the rest.

The best advice I can give people preparing to take plant medicine is that they need to expect the unexpected. Expectations are of the mind. Expectations are a killer. I cannot tell you anything about what you are going to experience. All I can say is that, whatever you are expecting - it's not going to be that. That's the start of us working together.

I use bits and piece of the Bwiti religion. It's probably considered cultural appropriation but what a stupid phrase! Our whole way of life we have culturally appropriated from this, that and everything. There is the truth and there is bullshit. If something feels like the truth, I will use it. I use; the Bwiti music, their resurrection supper which is chicken and rice, and the Bwiti prayer which people read out loud before and after ceremony. I use the word 'Basse' which is such a wonderful word, because translated it means, "this moment is the truth."

Regarding the current mainstreaming of plant medicines – I thought for a moment there, that we could combine and share information and ceremonial practices that worked - shamanistic traditions, but I went to the 'Beyond Psychedelics,' conference in 2018 and quickly realized it was just full of egos. There was only one guy coming from his own experience – an Australia guy, called Benjamin Mudge. He was the only one sharing from his own experience of healing his own mental illness with ayahuasca.

I quickly realized that the medical profession is just about making money. If a psychotherapist heals someone, they lose a client, so it's definitely not a good business model for them. It's a crock of shit. They are not interested in healing people - they are in business. I am the only person responsible for my own consciousness, nobody else; not my therapist, not my mother, not my shaman, not my doctor nor my religion.

The underground will remain as it always has - no need to move forward, if you are ready, you will find it and undergo an amazing psychic transformation and discover a world full of wonder and self-discovery.

In general, I will only work with conscious people who have already done a lot of work on themselves. Currently I am about to work with three siblings who say they have had a curse on them. It was a voodoo curse put on them by a jealous auntie. They are mid to late 50s - Africans from Trinidad. Of the three coming, two are twins. This is a new field of exploration for me using The Wood.

There is definitely an evolutionary component going on with regard to plant medicines. Early in 2010, when I was taking a lot of medicine, the people involved were part of the awakening movement. We were all on the same page and now, ten years later the plant medicines are potentiating a deeper level of collective awakening. They are waking people up to a different way of life. The medicines have bought people together from all cultures, religions, and belief systems and are committed to teaching; love, community, truth, consciousness, and sovereignty. We will see what clarity the Wood will bring to them. I will support them in their exploration but they are ultimately responsible. It is between them and the intelligence/consciousness of the blessed Wood.

CHAPTER FIVE

Spam Spagnoli – 5Meo-DMT

ANOTHER DAY in GOD's OFFICE

Monday, 7:00am: The Local, Gymea Bay

"So, there's Farik, sitting cross-legged on a tatami mat before me: a late 20s millennial with a wispy moustache and ADHD, wearing an Andean poncho and mumbling mantras and affirmations mixed with TOOL lyrics. His mesa's on the ground nearby with a few bottles of Agua de Florida and Shipibo knickknacks, but what really stands out is the Tibetan singing bowl he's wearing over his head. As I light the glass pipe, he gongs the bowl and bathes in the reverberations as he inhales the toad medicine. Then he starts shaking from the inside, releasing a long, infinite vibration and this cry escapes from his lips and his eyes roll back into his head, flickering white. I grab the singing bowl as it falls off and he starts to slide down to the floor and goes into a 'full release.' His body spasms like he's coming, or drowning, or being reborn, right?"

"Hectic. And is that the most out there you've seen?" Sat Nam asks, biting into her egg and bacon burger. Nam's built like an African warrior crossed with Venus de Milo: blonde hair, white teeth, big hips and bravado. A splash of tomato sauce stains her white ceremony kaftan.

Not that long ago she was a suburban hair dresser. We ran ceremonies in her salon sandwiched in between a milk bar and a fish n chip shop.

"Not by a longshot. But he is kind of indicative of the Aussie initiate. One who knows, you know."

"So, I don't think I've ever asked you this, but how did you get to be a toad shaman, anyhow?"

We're both dressed in white, like early morning yoga instructors as the tradies around us dig into the brekky menu at the local café. We've been in four ceremonies over the last three days at the waterfront temple, almost 40 people. Holding space is big work, as one day becomes the next and then the next in the ceremony of life...

I like the big groups for the tribal support, the group mind, and the collective expression. But the privates are equally good for deep healing, which is definitely recommended if there's any PTSD. This work can be gruelling. It can be cathartic. It can truly be transformational. But most of all it will teach you about yourself, that beautiful mind and the ego which keeps us separate from the wego all around. God is in the spaces in-between.

"Well, I've been doing this work full-time for around six years now and I've served over three thousand people. But first off, 'shaman's' a loaded term. I don't call myself that, even though this work has strong elements of shamanism in it. It also draws upon Western therapeutic models, and more recent modalities like rebirthing. Which makes us more midwives or doulas than shamans."

Since working with me as a client on her deep trauma issues two years ago, Nam's moved from hosting me, holding ceremonies at her house, to assisting in ceremony, to today, starting as my neophyte apprentice. Somewhere in the middle of all that I sent her off to Africa to work with iboga and the ancestors for her healing and she's come back all Bwiti-warrior-set-the-world-on-fire. Basse!

Today's the next step client visits for the last one-on-one sessions around urban Sydney. Which will work well to give her more background and feedback and see a diversity of responses. I accepted Nam's request to apprentice because I trust her. I get asked a lot to mentor, or shadow in ceremony, and each one is an emotional load, on top of holding space for so many. So, an apprentice is a deeper level of commitment. Each one bears my lineage, teachings, and reputation. And hopefully my sense of the sacred play.

"So, Obi-Wan, tell me – what do I need to know?" Nam asks, turning to one side and pulling on her nicotine vape.

"Well… it's not all love and light. There's blood and guts, trauma, sorrow, grief. All of humanity is there and it's often too much to bear. Imagine mid-wiving thousands of babies. Each birth different, and yet within the same parameters. Each one a miracle. Each soul unique and yet what is revealed is the interconnected One of All Things. Endless nirvana. Timeless satori. Samadhi. And yet, too many people sit once or twice with toad medicine and experience the joy, the ecstasis, and they want everyone to feel this. Whoah, Nelly. Slow down, integrate your own experience, everyone already has this within them, just waiting for the time to reveal. This is not your typical psychedelic. It's not something you take: it reveals something you already are."

"Yeah, I get that, I do. It's like all we have to do is remember."

"It's the same with people serving toad medicine – we all need more experience, to see all the ups and downs in the wide spectrum of people's responses, the light and the dark. People need to form their own relationship with the medicine, and to work on their own shadow."

I'm digging into a Big Breakfast: baked beans, mushrooms, avo, hash brown and bacon and runny eggs, sunny side up. We've got three bookings today – 9am, 2pm and 6pm, with not much time between for travel – so this may be all we eat. Self-nurturing is my weak spot, but you can't give from an empty cup and all that.

"I like that, yeah. More feminine." Nam's working on her feminine 'cause the masculine warrior energy is strong in her, she's had to bring it out to survive. 'Lived it, survived it, healed it.' is her motto, and she's not shy about sharing her trauma story. Classic wounded healer archetype.

Me? Birth trauma, sure, classic dissociation, rich imagination, ADHD: all the Western labels for neurodivergent. Old school 90s bush-doofer, stepping beyond the known and initiated with LSD and the lineage of the hippies. What was it Willy Wonka said? Oh yeah: "We are the music makers. We are the dreamers of the dream." And that's all I've got for you. Its right about now people get nosy, want to know your personal stuff. Like, why do you serve this medicine? What got you into it? Well, I took it. I had the God experience, I understand it. I grok it. It changed me forever and now I hold space for others to awaken to their true nature.

"Look, the whole 'shaman' term is just a Western brand, after all. Mircea Eliade invented it in his classic anthropology book Shamanism in the 1950s, based on the Siberian word saman. Eliade applied it across the board to medicine men and women, some who work with plants, others with trance and dance, the whole shebang. Then the whole infantilized West–whose archetypal father and mother shamans had all been killed by Dominator Culture over the centuries, looked back at the indigenous mystics and intuitively recognised they had something they were missing. Add nature – which abhors a vacuum and all that – and what do we get?"

"Instagram shamans healing their wounds whilst hustling for the Man?" Nam snaps back, all sassy.

"Close. Or maybe it's the same thing: a generation of shamanauts coming online and reweaving the sacred pathways, the relationship with nature through her exo-pheremones, the psychoactive plants, fungi – and toads!"

We've finished breakfast and the second round of take-away coffees have arrived. "C'mon, it's time we hit the road."

"Or the toad," Nam jokes, scooping up her soy latte.

Monday, 9:00am: Near Eastlakes Shopping Centre

The Atomic Telephone's gospelling over the car stereo as we drive along the A1, sticking to the speed limit. We pull up opposite the client's house, a non-descript weatherboard on an equally non-descript street, not too far from the airport – and debrief.

"Did you every watch that tv show, Highway to Heaven, when you were a kid? Y'know, Michael Landon's like this literal angel who moves from place to place, smiling his pearly whites and just like, helping people on behalf of God? Well, that's what this job feels like when I'm urban shamanising from place to place. We arrive, we do this thing to people, and at the end, they're usually pretty ecstatic and have had a God-realization. Or not."

"Sounds a bit like a gigolo," Nam laughs, knocking on the door.

"Or a sacred prostitute, yeah. Tantrikas. We reveal the Divine. But we do it with toad medicine."

Telstra workmen are hoisted up around a telephone pole a few houses down, doing their thing. The garbage trucks have just been past and open lidded wheelie bins are scattered across nature strips. That was one of the definitions Eliade used for the shaman you know: technician of the sacred. We're all just God's tradies.

Nam looks at me all wistful. "Crazy, huh, that this is our life. That this is what we do now. Spam, I love this, so much."

"Monday, Sat Nam. This is just Monday, 9am. Welcome to the rest of your life."

The door opens and there's Ling, an Asian woman in her mid-30's. Meditator, no big trauma issues on her in-take form (where I screen for overall health and mental wellbeing and suitability for this work). No heart issues, blood pressure is fine, no other medications, no SSRIS, emotional-parental issues but no deep trauma. She's been referred from another local client – all of my work is word of mouth, down low, under the line.

Over the years I've worked in an amazing diversity of locations, in: houses, apartments, Airbnb's, high-rises, hotels, converted garages, in converted hair dressers salons, yoga rooms, farms, retreat centres, national parks, bush domes, by rivers, on beaches – all sound, safe and sacred containers... all around Australia and the world. The sacred is everywhere, and right now, dear reader, you have no idea what your neighbours are getting up to. But if you hear these soul-rattling screams like a mix between a jaguar orgasming and a human murder, well, it might just be the Divine within revealing itself in an urban toad ceremony. C'est la vie.

Ling settles us in the meditation room of some urban Buddhist temple. We're surrounded by three gold skinned Buddha statues on pedestals along one wall and an impressive life-sized golden Buddha standing in a side alcove. Ling sits cross-legged on a bolster on the floor while I run through the ceremony logistics.

"Today we're working with the medicine of the Bufo Alvarius toad, which lives in the north of Mexico in the Sonoran Desert and stretches over the border into Arizona. The toads aren't harmed in any way – they're picked up gently and the parotoid glands on the back of their neck are squeezed. The secretion dries on glass, all organic, and we get these golden flakes," I say, showing Ling the toad medicine, stored in a small jar.

"For the weight ratio its said that the active ingredient here, 5-methoxy-n-n, dimethyltryptamine, or 5-MeO-DMT, is one of the strongest psychoactives we know of in nature. The only thing as strong as 5, is you. If you hold on, if you fight it." Seen that too many times. The ego can retract to the limbic system and flail around, caterwauling, thumping, screaming, resisting. Or the ego can slip into the tranquil place as the drop becomes the ocean and the white light void is all there is...

Nam sets out a plastic salad bowl and some tissues to the side of Ling's yoga mat, in case there's any purging. She smudges the room with some white sage then sits back down next to me on a cushion, opposite Ling.

I've set up my altar at the far end of the room, laying out a small square Shipibo tapestry as the base. There's a metal bell, chunks of Palo Santo to rest the glass pipes on, torch jet lighters, a tuning fork, a giant crystal shard, my Snaggletooth action figure from when I was seven, a large shell from Tiburon Island, sacred land to the Seri of Mexico, mapachos, white sage, a half empty bottle of golden agua de floridia, a singing bowl. Another layer of magickal items that come and go with Wu, holding charge for a while before moving on. In modern academic psychedelic discourse, it'd probably be called a syncretic, post-colonial neo-shamanic mash up.

"As the medicine comes on it's like a cork comes off a bottle and any energies that have been trapped or imprinted on the emotional body, the luminous light body, all those traumas and denser energies can be released. But all that's sort of the periphery of cleaning out to reveal the thing behind the ego mind, the Kingdom that lies within. Buddha nature. Christ consciousness. Samadhi. Just let go, as the drop remembers it's the ocean once more..."

The bell rings once, twice, three times:

"And so, we open this temple with great gratitude, for all that has come before. For Great Spirit which runs through all things, we ask today, for your strength, your wisdom, your love and your grace. Help us to remember Who – and What, We Really Are!"

It's a non-denominational opening–there's ceremonial aspects about holding space that I like, and having a delineated opening and closing is essential to the work and creating a safe container.

Holding space shouldn't be a confusing concept. There's no such thing as a spectator in ceremony – every look, every energy is felt and contributes to the whole. Holding space is mindfulness: we stay present. We protect the room. We allow what needs to express in the container of the ceremony and we do so without judgement. People may get nude, tear their clothes off, howl and scream, purge and vomit, or just cry and need to be held, and loved. And the space stays held.

Now, I didn't learn this from any one person. I drew from other facilitators and peers I've sat with over the years, seeing different styles. Everyone may serve differently, but a safe, sound and sacred space is the common denominator. I was initiated by a Mexican doctor who taught me what not to do, as much as what to do; but I've also sat with many masters and maestras, indigenous and Western, shamans and therapists. Some who formed their own entheogenic churches in the States, early adopters as this medicine started to come back into the modern psychedelic movement in the early Noughts.

Even though science has known that 5-MeO was in the Bufo Alvarius toad since the 1960s, it was only in the mid-1980s that Albert Most promulgated awareness of the medicine in his infamous pamphlet, which introduced The Church of the Toad of Light and gave instructions on the milking of the amphibian.

Which brings us back to Ling:

I've loaded up the handshake round – a small amount of this very powerful medicine. You can see the golden toad flakes through the clear glass of the bubble pipe. Ling takes three deep breaths, then as she exhales the final time, I light the pipe. She takes slow and gentle sips, holds it – and she's gone.

Well, sort of – she's still sitting up in lotus position, perfectly still. In the corner of the room my tiny black square Bose speaker is playing these looping Deya Dova icaros that layer the space with a soft, feminine presence, backtracking the interior journey. The buddhas stare down; everyone is implacable.

The moment goes on. And on. A sense of grace descends on the room.

"It-I-I am the universe, the whole universe is within me," Ling says, eyes still closed, perfectly still, like a zen-mannequin.

And then she screams.

Monday, 12:30pm: Heading north on the M1

"Hectic," Nam says, exhaling a stream of nicotine then dragging on her vape again, "I thought those screams were gonna bring the police down on us for sure."

"Trust in Allah and tie up your camel. Close the windows, turn up the music, and send out love and light. And remember, we're just midwives. There's always some noise rebirthing, just get your story straight. Now, listen…"

We're crossing lanes in the traffic while my GPS buffers to catch up on the phone. "Jenny's up next. In her 50s, meditator, energy worker. Wants to unblock her creativity. Have a look at her intake form," I say, motioning towards the phone.

We pass over some historic bridge into north Sydney adorned with Anzac statues and mild-afternoon traffic. Joggers cut along the parks, passing lovers on strolls, babies in prams, dogs on leashes: Peak Simulation.

"So, like, I wanna know, then. I get it that not everyone has the same experience, but it's the same space, yeah?" The tip of her vape pen glows as she drags on it.

"Well, yeah. I believe its where we come from, and where we go back to, that Zero Point behind everything. We all have it within us, but we all have a different path to unravel and reveal and remember it. The toad's just the training wheels. The kingdom lies within."

"So, apart from the gong head guy, what's the craziest thing you've seen in ceremony, then?"

"Hard to say. Each one's sacred, and unique. It really is like birthing souls and there's so many memorable moments. Great Moments in Toading, I call them! The gratitude rounds with the groups are probably my favourites. They're like hug doses; people have done the smaller handshake and slipped into the experience, then had a full release – which sometimes they don't remember if they fully let go – like a nirvakalpa ("no mind") state. And as the ego layer drops in all the individuals simultaneously, it's like the same ocean is revealed in everyone, interconnected – all the universe is there in one elongated peak moment – we're all one Great Being, every/ look /gesture /movement all choreographed in a fractaling-mirroring, karmic capoeira-like dance of consciousness..."

"You really do have a way with words, don't you?"

"Why do you think I'm called Spam?"

"And what about the other side? In the Bwiti tradition they say that the tree that reaches to heaven has its roots in hell."

"Yes. Well, for everyone that has an ecstatic liberation there's a potential for an equally ego terrifying breakthrough – or breakdown. Isn't that what happened to the author, Michael Pollan as recounted in his book, How to Change Your Mind? The ego that holds on, breaks. People purge, shake uncontrollably, all the trauma can come up, but they don't aways let it all go. Sometimes holding space can be dynamic, like a rodeo, and you really have to hold on for dear life. Other times you don't even notice what's happening right in front of your eyes.

"Cindy was like that. There–it's that flat on the corner, let's find a park," I say, gesturing to the art deco-lite building on the right.

"Who's Cindy?"

I pull over in the shade of a tree, behind a tradie's ute. I'm shaking. "The heart attack client.

"She had a thorough intake – more than usual as she was a cancer patient. I researched all the meds, nothing contraindicating. But she was on statins. And I think that weakened the heart when the bufo interacted. She seemed totally fine, just a tingling in her arms. Now that can happen on the medicine – you get an energetic snapshot of any blockages, tension, where something needs to be released. Cindy had a deep dive ¬ – but in the days afterwards she ended up with heart flutters and checked into hospital. They couldn't find any damage, but they think it was a mild heart attack. She was very lucky and she recovered. But it was a timely reminder of the dangers of this work. And the need to be vigilant."

"Whoooah, now that's hectic, brother."

"That's right. This is the real deal. You get it now. It's not just the toad medicine – they're here for us, too. Our experience. Our insight. Our ability to guide them safely through what in many ways equates to a near-death or mystic experience. To bungee-jump into the mind of God, and to come back, aware of who and what you really are. Alright. Jenny awaits. Let's give her our full attention, shall we?"

Monday, 2:00pm: Gladesville

Jenny's in 'full release' down on the floor, in her underwear, covered by a light blanket. She's purged half a dozen times into a silver salad bowl – mainly saliva, long drooling rivulets that we helicopter parent around, trying to catch as she tosses to and fro. It's just trapped energy she's releasing, nothing too solid.

To help clear that out Sat Nam and I share a handshake dose pipe of toad, letting the medicine curl down the throat and clear away the egoic rigidity. Like Peruvian ayahuasqueros when they first learn to drink the vine, it can be overwhelming. but when you're training to work with the medicine, to let it guide you, very small doses help tune into the ceremony. So too, with toad. As the ego lowers, the intuition heightens. And you still function around the room. It's Mexican style – frowned upon in the Western therapeutic model I'm sure, but everything has a place – as long as it's in service to the client. Who currently is cooing like a pigeon and thrashing urgently from side to side, giving off Stan Grofian-birth matrix vibes and flapping her hands into infinity.

Jennys's alternating between the maiden, mother and crone while Nam and I cradle her body as it flops around and she arches her back and goes into this ear splitting, orgasmic crescendo, a GODgasm that shakes the small flat. Outside the balcony window there's a roundabout on the corner. An endless stream of cars zip by, can they see? Could they even comprehend if they did?

As Jenny comes like a wave back to shore, falling back into her pillows and quietening, Nam touches her hand and something sparks between them, an energy. And Nam feels everything Jenny felt. In all the cosmic glory. And as her defences – and inhibition – go down, the Bwiti warrior comes out. Raging.

"Aggghhhhyoufuckinnngg*@*#*$$*s!!!!!!!!!!!!!!!!!" She rips off all her clothes – and I do mean all – and is doing some haka-style warrior dance whilst screaming revenge on the cunts that raped her as a child. Sympathetic purge for the Planetary Feminine in a corner flat in Gladesville. It's that full on. Didn't see that coming for the 2pm session, I'll admit.

I have one foot pressing down, anchoring Nam's foot, as I catch her eye and slowly calm her, horse-whispering her down. "Sat Nam, not here, not now, you've won that battle, you've 'Lived it, survived it, healed it.' remember? Come back to us, Nam, we need you here, holding space. Thank you."

"Oh shit," Nam falters... realizing where she is, what's happening.

We breath and just stare deeply into each other's eyes until the beast is back in the cage. She's panting heavily as I pass her the rattle and let her shake out all rage of women, all the bad things that have been done. Sometimes we surrogate for the client, or the collective. Sometimes it's ours, sometimes it's not. Somehow, perfectly though, it usually fits. And what happens in the ceremony stays in the ceremony. Storms over.

I kneel back down to Jenny, who's still weaving in and out of the white light and cries out to be held, so I stare deep into her eyes, the mirror to the soul. Connected. Safe. Reborn.... And as I hold Jenny in my arms, a song births:

Thank you, Great Spirit, waka na na nay - Thank you, Great Spirit, waka na na nay - Thank you, Great Spirit, waka na na nay - Thank you, Great Spirit, waka na na nay

I'm shaking the Peruvian wood rattle rattle rattle rattle rattle rattle rattle, and blowing agua de forida.

Thank you, Great Spirit waka na na nay - Thank, you Great Spirit waka na na nay - Whispering now: Thank you, Great Spirit, waka na na nay

This ain't my first rodeo.

Monday, 5:30pm: Randwick, I think...

We pull into a servo to fill up the tank and grab an iced coffee. There's more tradies in the line, all of us on our jobs across town.

"Look, it's all about them, not us. We're not trying to draw attention to what we need or feel called to do in ceremony," I begin. "In the therapeutic model it's called an intervention. In toad doulaing it's the same ¬– do we need to touch, or be seen, or intervene in any way? Yes, of course, sometimes – that's service. But knowing when and when not to, and when it's your thing that's unprocessed and coming out – that's the mastery. Sure, if they need a hug, or drool wiped, or help purging, or feathering a point gently to brush energy off, or mapachoing for cleansing... Sometimes a hand in the right spot can support, or restrain – there's a thousand variations on what can happen in ceremony. It's not a Western therapist's office. It's a higher-vibrational-rebirthing-container where the craziest shit can happen because it needs to, whether its orthodox or not."

"I fucked up, didn't I?"

"Yes. But that's how you learn. And she was fine with it, one tantric yoga priestess to another, sister. But we sure were lucky. Okay?"

"Okay. What a fucking day. I can't believe I did that. I'm so sorry."

"Well, it was on my watch as much as yours, y'know. Now listen: we still have the 6pm session in Maroubra. The day isn't over yet. You were built for this, remember?"

"Basse!" Nam grins with that same shit eating smile plastered across her face.

Deep breath. Here we go.

Monday, 6:00pm: Maroubra Beach

We exit the elevator directly into a modern, utilitarian apartment: high ceilings, beach view on the corner of the promenade. Behind glass doors on the corner balcony is Satan: a lean, muscled Doberman that snarls as he sizes us up, long teeth drooling with the anticipation of a kill.

"I rescued him from the pound when he was a puppy," Dante says proudly, waving him away through the glass. The beast settles on a worn matt and starts gnawing on a foot of thick garden hose, ripping and pulling it into rough plastic shards whilst staring at passers-by on the street down below and barking aggressively.

Dante's in his mid-30s, tall, dark, Mediterranean, with haunted eyes. His gym buddy Gabriel is one of the most built brick shithouses I've seen: chest as wide as a barrel, tatts, silver hair like a fox, calm grey eyes. He's been around, done some time for some shit, that's for sure. But both of them have a good energy, light, focused, ready to work with the toad. They're already medicine people.

"Ayahuasca saved my life," Dante says as we set up the room, laying some blankets and pillows down, smudging, setting up altars. Some people walk into a room and look for where the exits are. I look for the salad bowls (for purging), tissues, and for where I can put my altar. And then the exits. "I mean, I was so fucked up, drugs, alcohol, women, all coping mechanisms. I was literally killing myself and I was going off the rails. But my brother here, he brought me to the ceremony. To Madre. And she kicked my ass, big time."

"And now you bring me to the toad, full circle, bro." Gabriel smiles. He's rock solid. And packing shit. You can always see it on their faces. "I won't lie to you, bro, I'm packing shit," Gabriel says.

"I know. It's perfectly normal. It's the same as they say with ayahuasca – just surrender. But with 5-MeO, even the thought of surrender is just the mind having another thought. True surrender means letting go of everything, especially the mind – we call it a 'full release.' In Mexico they say: la dissolution finale."

Flash forward> Dante starts purging uncontrollably on the handshake round; Gabriel hardly feels anything at all. Which means he's got a high tolerance, or those adrenals are pumping out cortisol that can counteract tryptamines in the system, or at least with ayahuasca as it moves through the gut. Either way, there's no point making him more anxious by waiting, so as we land the handshake round, I prepare a big dose for the Gabriel's round two: 100mg.

Don Augustin Rivas is on the playlist. All the maestros on hot dial. The spirits sing. All the attention is on this moment, as the pipe lights and the crackling toad flakes combust, and the essence of the thing transfers from the lungs to the brain, inviting the electrical activity in the frontal and parietal lobes to cease. Gabriel takes in the whole pipe like a champ; he stays in lotus for a few moments then this look ripples across his face – shock? Awe? Understanding? And he falls gracefully back onto the blanket, perfectly still like buddha with a square cut jaw.

Dante, Sat Nam and I just hold space for the next 15 minutes, watching Gabriel's chest rise up and down, the slight twitches of tension and release on his enormously tattooed arms, the endless aura of equanimity in his entire being, given over to something bigger, loving, radiant and eternal. Nam starts to get her feather out like she wants to clear some energy and she's reaching for the small hand drum, but I wave her off. He's perfect as he is, he doesn't need us. Let the masculine be...And then he's back, all smiles and eyes aglow, like he knows now, in ways that words cannot express. And he's brought some of that ocean of light back with him into his drop.

Dante's turn is decidedly darker. After the handshake, he confided: "My family are from Turkey, this little village, and something bad happened there. They all died, on this hill. There was a massacre. Madre showed it to me: men, women and kids, innocents – they were all killed. I don't know if my ancestors were the ones who killed or were killed, but this energy is in me like a cloud and its real dark, bro. It's heavy and dark and I-I... I can't hold onto it anymore, it comes out of me, it wants to rain." And then he cried.

I pack him another big round: 75mg, and he purges almost immediately. Dry wracking heaves squeezing in peristalsis, cleaning out his system and tapping back into the entire karmic line. Sat Nam's shaking her drum and singing this higher vibrational light language into him as I swap bowls and rinse his purge in the kitchen sink, blocking it irrevocably. Dante's wrapped in the angelic feminine, shaking out his darkness, as Sat Nam dances around him. I light a mapacho and soplar his back, feet and head as he hangs there over the bowl, emptying out. Smoke curls around him in tantalizing shapes, faces, spirits.

Gabriel gives him water as Sat Nam sits Dante up. We lock eyes. "Three deep breaths, then gently sipping," I say, and start lighting the second big round of toad. Dante gulps it down and looks at me with the eyes of drowning man: inescapable, pulled down the whirlpool. And then he's gone. Each time the medicine hits his system it finds the darkness within, and he purges, again and again and again as I chase him with the glass salad bowl, filling with the raspberry smoothie he had for lunch and an endless river of karmic bile and death all mixed together.

Dante's screaming and purging and choking on his own vomit and we turn him on his side as he screams and purges again. Sat Nam launches into action with her drum::: the heartbeat :::: the anchor point : something to hold onto in the storm. And she's channelling spirits and ancestors and Bwiti chants into him, we're all holding him, Gabriel's shadowing with pillows – and at the crux of the energetic wave I turn and see–

Satan, perfectly still, staring right at us, his eyes imploring, and for some reason something just gets a hold of me and I go to the glass door and try to pull the handle just as–

Nam screams: "Spam, no! That dog's a killer – look at its eyes! It'll eat your face!!!"

Satan's barking and scratching at the glass, whinnnnnnningggg and then he stares straight at me, and that's not a dog, man. Its heavy. There's a whole village in there.

There's death in those eyes – and teeth. An ancient hunger has been stirred up. All that darkness was too much for Dante to bear alone – so the dog became the energetic overflow. All those bodies in the village, the dark mountain, night forest. All the little deaths that pass down through time and leave a shadow on our children's children.

And then I'm back in my body, shaking the wooden rattle, Nam's singing her Bwiti chants, Dante's still purging but his body's stopped shaking; he's coming back. We're all of us coming back, what the fuck– The Maroubra Beach exorcism has peaked. I look at Nam and she looks at me and we just laugh.

"What were you thinking, Spam!?" That dog would've killed us!" she says between guffaws.

"You're totally right," oh god, now I've got the giggles. "Please, do a clearing on that dog. And hand me a mapacho!"

Monday, 11:00pm: Coogee Bay Road, Coogee

"I bet Michael Landon could manifest a car park in Coogee late at night," Nam jokes, as we circle the block for like the third time. "Wait – there's one." Indecipherable council bylaw rules on the sign and a ridiculously small wedge of space between two Teslas on the main street.

"Man, it's a reverse park. I don't think there's enough room. I'll try –

"Yoda says—"

"There is no try. That's my line. But I'm freaking exhausted. Man, I just can't angle it. I'm done."

Nam looks at me all wistful. "You did good today."

"Well, so did you."

"My God, I mean – I learned so much. And I've still got so much to learn."

"That you do. So, today was the peak experience, but the real work ahead is the integration. Making sense of what was revealed. The clients will be doing that – we've sent them the integration document, and we remain open for them as questions and memories arise. We're always connected. Oh, and Natasha has an integration dinner set up for next week, see if you can go, I'll post the link to you later."

Nam isn't my first apprentice, or mentee, or assistant, or host, but it sure does feel good to know that a new generation is blooming. That being a medicine carrier can" reweave the sacred bonds between us, nature and God. That there's a whole network of us out there, made up of everyone that has felt the vibration of the revelation. All of us in service to the call.

"We're all students on the path, Nam – but we're not alone. We're not separate. One drop's awakening entrains the pool. All of us, healing, receiving, shining." I flick on the hazard lights and unbuckle my seatbelt. "Ok, apprentice, you're going to have to park it for me."

"Oh, fuck all right – get out," Nam says with a grin, and executes a perfect three step slide to the curb.

I get my suitcase out of the back of the car, sling my medicine bag over my shoulder, and we trek along towards Harry's place, a block up for midnight steaks and decompression. The stars shine down on us through a cloudless night.

"The Bwiti, the pygmy people that brought iboga to the world, they have a saying: Thank you, Lord, for today. The first, the last and the only day we get," Sat Nam smiles.

Just another day in God's office.

CHAPTER SIX

Pip – Psilocybin Mushrooms

My Grandfather was the archetypal sage - the pipe, the long silver hair, the weathered face and a twinkle in his eye. He had carved his niche in the sprawling city of Sydney, as the founder of a magical order known as the O. P. A., dedicated to the esoteric arts of the Western tradition. His reputation among those who dabbled in the occult, preceded him, and he was often surrounded by a curious tribe from the fringes of society, eager to share his wisdom.

One fateful day, as a curious and impressionable 14-year-old, I ventured into his humble unit within the confines of a retirement village. The stark contrast of the mundane exterior of the seniors' community and the aura of mystery and magic that enveloped him, was nothing short of surreal. As I stepped onto his veranda, I noticed an unassuming plant placed in front of a trough of geraniums. My grandfather and his boarder, a gentleman in his twenties, were huddled over it, their voices hushed in intimate conversation. The scene was like a tableau from some forbidden ritual.

Curiosity piqued; I couldn't resist inquiring about the significance of the herb. Grandad turned to me, a mixture of concern and amusement dancing across his weathered face. "Oh, that's sage," he replied, with a depth to his words that hinted at something special.

Driven by an inexplicable impulse, I pressed further, daring to ask, "Is it a special sage?" The atmosphere became charged and all eyes turned towards me. My grandfather regarding me with a mixture of surprise and curiosity. I realized I had inadvertently stumbled upon a well-guarded secret. That moment possibly marked the beginning of my journey into the world of plant medicine - and that sage was something I'd seek out again over the next few years.

As it was in the early days of the internet, you had to connect your internet cable to the home phone line, and with there being only one shared family computer in a communal area, I had to be quick. "SPECIAL SAGE" I typed into the search bar, hoping something would come up. I sifted through recipes and gardening blogs until I hit the jackpot - a site called 'Erowid.' This site would become a valued ally in my searches over the coming years.

Salvia Divinorum – a divinatory psychedelic. I knew I needed to get my hands on some but didn't dare ask my grandfather, after the way he reacted to my inquiry. I hadn't a clue where to find it, being the 14-year-old daughter of a Navy Commander and a church going nurse and attending an uppity, North Shore Sydney, private girl's school. My parents didn't even approve of me visiting my eccentric grandfather alone, let alone traipsing around town unchaperoned, looking for exotic psychedelics (not that I told them).

My hunt for this mysterious herb ended up on the backburner until years later when I was at university and heard a friend talking about something called; 'The Silk Road.' He claimed that for a mere twenty bucks he could procure me a small bag of this herb. So of course, I took him up on his offer.

A few weeks later, I was sitting in the bedroom of my future husband's parent's house, pipe in hand, shaking with anticipation. As the red ember slid through the metal bowl, I was pushed into something I can only describe as having the energy of an upside-down beach - but not actually an upside-down beach. I felt a heavy weight across my chest and was pushed by force into the bed... or so it appeared. It was an interesting experience but nothing too mystical. However, it made me realise that the human mind was far less rigid than I had initially thought.

Years passed with a multitude of psychedelic fuelled adventures. From microdots of LSD in Byron Bay, to mushrooms in Cambodia, from Ketamine in India to 2CB in Katoomba, with a bit of Huachuma directly from the Mercado de Bruja (Witches Markets) in Bolivia, sprinkled in too. But my real calling to the medicine began around the time that two good friends introduced my husband and I to the art of foraging for Psilocybe Subaeruginosa, a particularly potent mushroom, in the pine forests of NSW.

This coincided with a time that my life was falling apart. I had just detoxed from hard drugs in an inpatient rehab. Although I was now clean from drugs, I experienced a massive void. I soon began drinking alcoholically and developed an eating disorder. I had constant suicidal thoughts and a strong victim mentality. Spending time in the forest, foraging for mushrooms became a sacred endeavour, and one of the few places I found some solace from the chaos and fallout of my hedonistic existence.

I complained to my friend that I just couldn't seem to find happiness. She replied, "I know you've taken psychedelics, but have you ever taken them with intention?" "No" I said blankly, not really knowing what she meant. I had nothing to lose, so that week my husband and I ground up 9 grams of handpicked, dried Psilocybe subaeruginosa. We divided it in half and took it with some lemon juice.

I lit a candle, ran a bath, and jumped in. I'd set the intention of self-compassion. As the bathwater turned into a thick soup, I was transported to a place where love ceased to exist - a mechanical realm with no humanity. I was all that was left of humanity and I had never felt so scared and lonely. The separation from love felt horrific. I felt so terribly empty and could not escape this place. Then from somewhere in the back of my mind, a voice said; "You need to BE the love." Becoming love in a place of such isolation and fear felt impossible. The concept of love had become so foreign, I didn't even know what I was trying to muster.

As I tried hard to focus my attention on the people I remembered loving, in what felt like a distant reality – images of my husband, my parents, and my sister flitted into my mind's eye. This began to slowly spark a fire and love began to flow. I was able to find love, even for this hellscape. The moment I did this, my life changed forever. A stream of light and a golden lotus burst forth from the crown of my head. It had billions of petals emanating from the centre of itself. In the middle was a beautiful being - the most beautiful being I'd ever witnessed.

I couldn't see them, but I could feel their energy. I didn't need to see them - they were pure love. I felt a lifetime of gratitude just being in their presence. There were arms all around me; hundreds of arms each with an eye in its hand - each hand emanating the same love as the being. The more gratitude I felt, the more beautiful it became until I was in a state of pure ecstasy - in awe of this ever-loving presence. This went on for what felt like two hours, a feedback loop of me feeding her gratitude as she engulfed me in a shower of love, compassion and beauty.

As I came to, my husband said that the entire time I'd been chanting the word "YAM." I learned that this is the mantra for the heart chakra. I immediately started searching for answers, as I intuitively felt that I was probably not the first person to have experienced this. I came across a Tibetan text which spoke of Avalokitesvera the bodhisattva who contains the compassion of all Buddhas, and has 1000 hands of Compassion and an eye of Wisdom in each palm, just as I'd seen. I learned that Avalokitesvara is also an emanation of Kuan Yin - the goddess of compassion who emerges from a lotus and is associated with the heart chakra and the seed mantra, I'd been chanting the entire time. I was certain that I had been graced with this divine presence and in the weeks that followed, I would carry her sacred healing into my life.

What followed was nothing short of a miracle. As quickly as I'd fallen, I was reborn. My insatiable craving for the next thrill was replaced by a profound stillness. My yearning for a substance to numb my pain, was replaced by the sobering realization that I had to confront my pain head on. In this brave confrontation I began to discover what it meant to truly live.

I waited for the fall, but it never came. My pain had been removed and in its place was magic. Magic and the understanding that I had a choice. I could go back to being a drunk, unhealthy, miserable wretch or do something with my life. And for the first time in 15 years, I actually chose the latter. Don't get me wrong, what followed was a lot of integration, rawness and humility that comes from taking a personal moral inventory, as suggested in the AA and NA, 12 step programme. At times this work seared into me like a hot poker and made me question whether the effort was worth the reward. The realisation that the pain of accountability was absolutely necessary, was like a smack in the face, but it served me well.

Years of doing medicine work followed and the subsequent integration propelled me from the loneliness of victimhood to personal liberation. I felt like I had been gifted a magic key – the key to fulfillment and I had no choice but to share my gift with others. I returned to studies, something I had previously sworn off, after graduating from five tumultuous years at university in 2014. I set about becoming a holistic therapist.

Assisting people to have their own empowering journeys felt like a natural step in the direction of my calling. But it wasn't until I started offering psychedelic integration, that I discovered my true calling. For years this was something I had just done naturally, helping friends, acquaintances and strangers navigate their psychedelic experiences, whether that be; preparation, supporting their journeys or integration afterwards. They would run their otherworldly experiences by me as we endeavoured to identify and extract the gold nuggets.

I volunteered at several festivals and ran integration circles so people could work through some of their medicine induced shifts in consciousness. I just naturally fell into this work. Combined with my understanding of various types of psychotherapy and other healing modalities, I've had the privilege to witness some profound transformations in many lives.

While my preparation and integration work allowed me to show up passionately and authentically and was aligned with my own personal path, I knew I could be doing more. I sensed that I was being called to facilitate - but I was scared. I knew the medicine inside out - I had witnessed its magic, wisdom and grace many times over. In fact, I understood the medicine more than I understood most people. It spoke to me in the forest, in my daily life, and in my dreams. I was constantly asked by clients, how I felt about facilitating. Every time it was mentioned, I felt a familiar prickling behind my eyes and a buzzing through my body. But I suppressed it.

All of a sudden, the floodgates opened and I started weeping. I would weep for all the people who were living a life of suffering, knowing that I had an antidote but was too afraid to share it with them, because of my fear of repressive authority and the law. It was then that I called upon God, The Universe, or whatever you want to call it - for guidance.

Through a divine chain of synchronicities, some of the most influential people on my journey, were placed into my life, right when I needed them. People who had walked this path before me. People who understood the power of this medicine and wanted nothing more than to see it weave its healing magic through the world. I give massive credit to both Julian and Dale (both of whom you will be familiar with from this book) who imbued the wisdom of their experience onto me and helped alleviate my fears, as I began the journey of facilitating.

I've also been lucky enough to have had the support of a handful of other facilitators, who out of respect for their privacy, I cannot name. They guided me onto this path and assisted me in finding my feet. Each facilitator had a unique approach in working with these medicines. Through my experience, I've honed a method that feels harmonious for both the client and myself. I feel it's important to choose a facilitator, who has a deep personal relationship with the medicine and who works in a way that is in alignment with your values.

Most people discover underground facilitators via personal recommendation, typically whilst seeking alternative options after many traditional methods have failed them. While I'd love to operate with complete transparency, the current climate requires discretion. While there are dedicated individuals and organisations striving to make this field more accessible - at the time of this writing, the use of psychedelics for therapy remains constrained by stringent guidelines, exorbitant costs and a plethora of legalities.

My work with clients usually starts with an initial fifteen-minute phone call where I briefly discuss what they can expect in a session - the risks and benefits, contraindications and what such a commitment might mean for them. It is a time for us to see if we gel and could work together. It provides the opportunity to answer a few questions. Upon agreeing to work together, I schedule a preparatory call. This hour-long session allows me to gain a deeper understanding of their unique needs, ensuring they receive tailored support throughout their journey. It helps the client to gain insight into their needs, and prepare more fully for the upcoming therapeutic work.

It's important that the client selects a comfortable environment. Many prefer their own home as it's their safe haven and place where they can be the most open and vulnerable. Those travelling from greater distances, might opt for hotels, cabins, or Airbnb's. On the day of the medicine session, I ask them to fast for three hours minimum and recommend that they extend the fast to social media and other forms of negative distractions. I understand that this is often a very big day for them and so I do what I can to alleviate their fears. I find that those who are nervous, usually hold a deeper respect for the medicine and it in turn responds more gently. On the other hand, those who come in with too much ego and confidence are often put in their place by the wise, playful sentience of the mushroom.

I encourage the client to sit with the mushroom tea and stir in their intentions before drinking it. This forges a connection between them and the mushroom spirit which will act as gatekeeper, guide, and therapist as they traverse the intersection between self and spirit together. This next 4-6 hours is usually spent in an introspective journey through the paradigm of existence, allowing the client to forge a deeper understanding of themselves and their place in the universe. During this time, it's important that I, as facilitator, remain present enough so that the client feels safe and cared for, but not insert myself into their experience. This could potentially pull them from a journey of deep healing and exploration.

As the client rouses from their inner journey, they will often attempt to explain the awe they have witnessed, but they soon realise the ineffability of such a profound experience.

Integration is important - this "mining the gold" from the experience and forging it into something tangible within the seeker's life. This is particularly useful in the case of healing unhealthy patterns or trauma associations which play out in their lives. I recommend they put the following day aside to focus on integration - making notes, talking to friends or loved ones, creating artwork or revisiting the music playlist from the medicine session to elicit their insights back into conscious awareness.

I organise a session for the following week to help solidify any insights and realisations and how they might use their newfound wisdom to create a blueprint that will act as a guide for real life change. As a therapist, I believe that structured integration is a valuable investment of time. There are several underground practitioners whom I deeply respect, who believe that the power of the medicine experience is enough. The multifaceted nature of this work is nuanced and there is definite space for, and value in, both schools of thought.

The potency of psilocybin in catalysing rapid and profound change is astonishing. The transformation that unfolds eclipses what one might expect to get from years of traditional therapy. Lifelong phobias - those invisible chains that bind people to their deepest fears, are broken, dissolved by this therapeutic alchemy. People teetering on the edge of despair, find a real lifeline. They discover a renewed meaning and zest for life. Fractured relationships that once seemed irrevocably damaged, find a pathway towards reconciliation and understanding.

I've had the privilege of witnessing people who once viewed themselves through a lens of judgment and inadequacy, emerge with a renewed sense of self-love and acceptance. Chronic anxiety, an all-too-common spectre of our times, has dissipated before my eyes, freeing individuals from its relentless grip. Even the heavy cloak of grief, caused by the loss of a loved one, is lifted, allowing space for remembrance and peace.

The emotional journeys traversed in plant medicine sessions are vast and varied, encompassing the full spectrum of human experience. Yet the common thread is the release and healing that comes from truly feeling and acknowledging these emotions. By creating a space where emotions can be experienced in their rawest form, psilocybin can facilitate a profound healing.

My dear friend and medicine worker, Dan Nguyen describes it thus; "Psilocybin-assisted therapy, in essence, mirrors a therapeutic dialogue with the most authentic version of yourself. As if you are both the seeker and the therapist. It is an exploration that delves into the intricacies of one's psyche, offering insights that are deeply personal and transformative."

During my time working with psilocybin mushrooms, I have had the privilege to witness so much deep healing. Stella is a client who comes to mind – a resilient and inspiring woman in her 30s who had lived with the ongoing burden of childhood sexual assault at the hands of a family member. She immigrated to Australia from the Philippines as a child. She experienced a constant, futile attempt to overcome a deep intergenerational father wound.

During her mushroom session, she was able to bridge the vast distance of her ancestral past, and heal the wounds carried from her father's lineage. It was a poignant reclamation of her cultural heritage, providing her with a newfound sense of connection and identity, and a deeper understanding of the perils that had descended through her paternal lineage. Stella was able to sever the emotional bonds to her father that were holding her back from the true expression of herself. She realised that looking for praise and acceptance from him was a futile endeavour and that she was worthy of a place in the world regardless. She experienced a sense of self-love, and acceptance that she carries with her still.

Under the guidance of the medicine, she relived a childhood sexual assault with courage and fortitude. Raised as a Catholic and indoctrinated by religious preaching on the topic of forgiveness, a concept that had remained illusory, distant, and abstract when it came to her abuser. She was able to arrive at a new concept of forgiveness and see it as an act of self-healing, not a concession to her abuser. Stella did what, had once seemed impossible - she forgave him – not as absolution for him, but for her own liberation. What resulted was a profound sense of release and empowerment as that significant barrier was removed. She repeatedly confides in me, the immensely positive influence the session had on both her personal healing and the healing of family relationships.

While the majority of sessions are positive, there was one that was unexpectedly difficult, not due to the mushrooms, but a logistical problem that arose. My client, Diana, deeply in tune with her spirituality and an experienced meditator, was looking to delve deeper. She lived in a tranquil, secluded bush setting, so the last thing we expected was any outside disturbance.

About an hour into the session, I heard incessant footsteps pacing on her veranda. Not wanting to disturb her, I went outside to investigate and found a young man pacing around muttering and in distress. He was saying a name repeatedly - which I eventually realised was the name of my client's partner. I also noticed that my car doors were open. Due to his distress and the fact I had no idea who he was, I deemed it necessary to disturb my client.

The startled and irritated Diana, gave me her partners phone number. She was annoyed that this situation had occurred on the one day she'd put aside for her experience. She was unsure of why this man was here, but knew who he was. Her partner was the man's carer and it turned out that he had absconded from the back seat of his car when he had returned to the house to drop something off. Her partner quickly returned and collected the guy, but the moment was lost. Diana was unable to fully surrender after this.

She was able to experience some somatic release and had an experience that mimicked being in the womb. Interestingly, she'd stated prior to the session that she had an intuitive sense that something was amiss and felt some invisible barrier present to her being able to surrender and fully experience the effects of the medicine. This exemplifies the sentience of the medicine and the power of intuition, which, is often discussed by those working from a shamanic worldview.

Psilocybin's transformative power cannot be overstated, especially for those battling treatment-resistant depression and persistent mood disorders. Its capacity to enhance cognitive processes and induce neuroplasticity is well-documented, but its impact reaches far beyond these tangible benefits and ventures into metaphysical realms. Psilocybin is a catalyst for profound spiritual awakenings. Even atheists will attest to an unexpected encounter to a spiritual force, which often leads to an expansive shift in their sense of interconnection with the world and imbues their lives with a newfound sense of meaning.

These spiritual revelations induced by psilocybin are usually life-altering. A single experience can reroute an individual from a path marked by existential emptiness to one overflowing with purpose and joy—a transition that many people seek, but rarely ever find. That psilocybin can facilitate such a fundamental shift in perception and identity is extraordinary.

Introducing someone to psychedelics for the first time never loses its magic. It's akin to possessing a small, enchanted chest and allowing the seeker a glimpse at its contents. Contents so full of mystery and magic that they are truly ineffable. Though the lid must be closed again and the chest tucked away, those who experience what lays inside are invariably transformed and leave with the profound knowledge that magic truly exists. Witnessing this metamorphosis, one experiences the essence of human adaptability and growth. This highlights the immense promise of psilocybin as not only a therapeutic agent but a key to unlocking a more purpose-driven existence.

I have witnessed an increasing demand for psychedelic therapy in the underground. Some label this time, the "psychedelic renaissance." The public is beginning to view psychedelics as the medicines they are, and the shackles of stigma are loosening. It's important for seekers to understand the power and sacredness of these plants. There is a risk that as psychedelics make the journey from the fringe to the mainstream, they will start to be treated with less sanctity and commodified in the same way that pharmaceuticals are. It's a double-edged sword. On the one hand it means accessibility to those who need them - while on the other hand there is the potential for commercial exploitation and a loss of their ancient scaredness.

It's important that practitioners don't look solely at these medicines as a way to fund the pharmaceutical oligarchy - but to learn from indigenous cultures who have a far deeper knowledge of sacred plants than what is quantifiable with scientific data. With the medicalisation of psychedelics, I feel that the underground has immense responsibility in emphasising the sacred relationship between humans and these medicines. I feel this is an important commitment for those stepping into facilitation in the underground.

In the unfolding narrative of the psychedelic resurgence, I stand at the crossroads of ancient wisdom and modern therapy, committed to preserving the sacredness of the psychedelic experience. The transformations I've witnessed are testament to the capacity of psilocybin to unlock emotional and spiritual depths that have remained untapped by conventional therapeutic methods.

As we collectively navigate the complexities of mainstreaming these medicines, and the increasing demand - maintaining our integrity is paramount. The delicate balance between accessibility and sanctity is the crux of the work ahead for facilitators like myself, who are determined to ensure that the soul of psychedelic therapy remains true to its sacred purpose. It's a profound privilege to accompany others on such a transformative path, and an honour to contribute to a global shift, towards deeper social and self-understanding and healing.

CHAPTER SEVEN

Nick S – Ayahuasca, Iboga, Kambo, San Pedro

I was interested in psychedelics from a young age, reading everything I could find about them from library books and the internet. I was around 12 the first time I heard about magic mushrooms from my older brother and I distinctly remember thinking, 'I will try those.' So, the curiosity was always in me. I was also a big fan of the Carlos Castenada books, Fear and Loathing in Las Vegas and The Electric Kool-Aid Acid test, all of which I devoured while I was still in high school. I first found out about Ayahuasca from a book by an Ayahuasca shaman that I found in the local library around this same time.

In my youth I was heavily into recreational psychedelics, taking them often at friend's houses, raves, warehouse parties, music festivals and in nature. It was a time of reckless experimentation. I was looking for something but wasn't sure what. At the age of 33, I had my first Ayahuasca ceremony and realized this was what I had been looking for all these years - there just hadn't been any cultural context for it when I was growing up, so I'd fallen into the party drug scene by default. I'd had some healing experiences during my youthful experiments, but the ceremonial container with healing intentions was the real game changer.

My intention for my first ceremony was to deal with a crippling death anxiety I'd had since youth. I wasn't sure where this came from, but I always had a fear of death that paralysed me on a regular basis. I'd heard Ayahuasca made you confront this. I was also quite blocked in my creative career as a comedian at the time, and thought it might help me artistically.

Looking back, I'd say I'd been seriously depressed since adolescence and when I discovered drugs, I began self-medicating regularly with cannabis, amphetamines, alcohol, psychedelics, MDMA and whatever exotic synthetic chemicals I could find, just no hard drugs. I didn't realise I was depressed at the time because it was how I'd felt since high school. I didn't realise there was another option. When I began healing, I realised how shut down and out of balance I'd previously been.

After my first three Ayahuasca experiences my depression significantly reduced and most of my major drug addictions faded away without even trying. The root had been removed. I was told by the medicine to abandon my standup comedy career and go do volunteer work instead. My life took an abrupt 360-degree turn. I was also no longer an atheist, as I experienced firsthand the spiritual worlds I'd read about in my youth. I'd always been spiritual seeker but this was the first time I directly experienced these realms to be 'real,' in a way that shook the very foundations of my soul.

On my fifth journey I connected with the spirit of my dead grandfather who had been a healer and medicine man in his village. I felt his latent DNA inside my genes switch on and suddenly realized that I could do this work and this was to be my path. After that, I became obsessed with all things to do with plant medicine and healing. During this same journey I had this intense connection with Source or Spirit – whatever you want to call it – whom informed me that we were in some kind of spiritual battle, and that anyone who had the capacity for this work was urgently needed to assist with the consciousness shift that was required during these chaotic times.

I ran from the calling for about eight months. I thought it was absolutely crazy to think that I could serve these medicines, mostly because of the level of self-work and training that I'd need to do in order to be a shaman/facilitator, but also because I didn't want to be responsible for other people that would be under my care. During this eight-month period, my life went to absolute shit and I realized there was no running away, this was it and so I began walking the path.

I began serving very early on. In hindsight I should have waited but I was on this evangelical mission to assist with the consciousness shift and so I just went for it after only a couple of years of working with it myself. I trained primarily with two mentors/teachers. One was following an eighth generation Peruvian Mestizo lineage and the other was entirely non-traditional DIY. They were pretty much the opposite of one another. One had lots of rules, the other had hardly any rules. I learnt a lot from both styles and I guess found myself somewhere in between the two, trying to find the underlying essence of plant medicine practices but free of any of the cultural baggage that didn't resonate with my own experience.

I started small - serving the medicine to anyone who came my way. My groups ranged from 1-10 people, mostly friends who knew each other. I didn't know what I was doing in the beginning but I learnt quickly. I honestly believe my innocence protected me during that early phase. Still there were a couple of situations early on where I feel I dosed a few people too high, too quickly and I learnt one of the most important lessons with medicine - You can always have more but you can never have less.

At this point, I only charged enough to cover the costs. I just loved the life and enjoyed the process. I was doing my own work simultaneously and often the two processes were intertwined. I gave many free healings as I believed the medicine should be available for everyone. I was a bit broke at the time so had empathy for people who struggled to pay for healing. I was very idealistic at this point and against the monetization of the medicine, but after encountering some really annoying situations involving projection and people unable to own their shit during free sessions, I realized there had to be some kind of energetic exchange (not necessarily money) otherwise the healing didn't stick or people were more likely to blame you for what was brought up.

Two years into serving, I started making a living from it. Medicine was my life and I wanted enough money to continue with my own healing and to get some more training so I could be better at my job. It was also hard to hold down a regular job while doing this work because it became an all-consuming passion. I lived and breathed it.

It's hard to balance the monetary aspect of plant medicine healing work, but it's a fact of life if you are still living in the Matrix. You have to check yourself regularly and make sure your intentions are always clear and not motivated by money or any personal agenda, because if you are not careful, the line can get blurry. Ultimately no amount of money is worth having to deal with a client who is not ready and after a couple of stressful situations early on, I'm more cautious, selective and have a better screening process.

My honeymoon phase is definitely over. In the beginning I thought I was a central focal point of change but I had a lot of ego inflation in those first few years due to the spiritual emergence process I was going through and the amount of medicine I was drinking. Now, I have no illusions about the nature of this work and consider myself just another employee for Spirit - doing my part for the healing and awakening of the world that hopefully happens before it's too late, while trying to deal with my own shit which never seems to end. I see myself as a middleman, or a bridge and the more I get out of the way of the process, the more the magic can happen.

I love all the medicines for different reasons. They all have their place in the canon and depending on the individual, their issues and where they are at in their healing journey, certain medicines are going to be more effective than others for them. I began with Ayahuasca and Kambo. That was my mainstay for the first 5-6 years. The changes I saw in people were incredible. Ayahuasca opened people up to spiritual realities and the cosmic self. I saw it heal many Western treatment resistant issues from neuro-fibromyalgia, cancer, rheumatoid arthritis, depression, anxiety, deep vein thrombosis and more.

Ayahuasca is very good at clearing the body, mind, spirit and emotions. It connects people to the divine feminine, to Spirit and to themselves. It's just so versatile and beautiful. Ayahuasca without a doubt, saved my life. It turned me around from a dark path I was heading down and woke me up. It reminded me of all the magic in the world; something that gets lost for many people stuck in the Western materialist paradigm. It helped me remember my spiritual self and experience it directly. I really loved the brewing process as well, exploring the use of different admixture plants to modulate the effects of the brew. There is a real art to making a perfectly balanced brew. It's almost like wine tasting, but more about the experience then the taste.

I saw Kambo treat many illnesses that were resistant to western treatment: Lyme disease, immune system disorders, chronic pain issues and more. Kambo is great for anxiety and depression because it brings people back into their bodies through ordeal. Kambo toughens people up and brings out the warrior. It is also helpful because you can take it while on anti-depressants and many other medications that are contraindicated with other plant medicines.

Kambo can help people get off psychiatric medications. It can clear many side effects of long-term use or withdrawal. There are underground protocols involving microdosing mushrooms and Kambo that can help people wean off psychiatric medications that would be impossible to get off without extreme withdrawal. I treated a man who had suffered for several years from the debilitating side effects of Lyrica. After two treatments they were all gone. People report tasting the medications on the back of their throats as they throw up, even after having stopped them for several years!

Kambo is a very useful medicine, its duration is short and rarely has any psychotropic effects. It's also useful preparation for other medicines as it accomplishes the physical cleansing aspect of the treatment, allowing the other medicines to go into the person on a deeper level. Giving people Kambo first was also my way of building trust and seeing how they'd react to uncomfortable processes and how they might react to the other medicines. It's very grounding and good for people who've become ungrounded after doing too many of the other higher chakra medicines.

I switched to facilitating Iboga after experiencing how incredibly healing it was, especially with early childhood core wounds. Wow. What a medicine. The ultimate medicine some may say! While Ayahuasca took me into the cosmos, Iboga took me deep into my soul. It showed me who I was and why I was the way I was. Unlike all the other tryptamines, Iboga really was about the base, sacral and solar plexus areas of the body. It took me far deeper than anything else I had tried. It just lasts so long, there is no chance of spiritually bypassing during an Iboga flood dose, unlike with some of the other plants.

Having worked in the Ayahuasca sphere for several years by that point, I saw how people could take it all the time to avoid dealing with their deeper stuff, but with an Iboga flood dose there was no escape. It is the ultimate shadow work plant that just did not let up until you'd faced your demons. This plant is the king of medicines, especially when dealing with addiction, core wound and childhood trauma work. It's like psychic open-heart surgery and requires a lot of preparation and safety, as it is the only plant that I know where someone can die under certain conditions.

People literally go back to being 3–5-year-olds, you can see the child in their face as their entire psyche comes undone, so you have to be very careful. Yet the rewards are just incredible. It's so grounding and takes a person out of their mind and back into their bodies. Iboga brings the wayward child into line. He grounds and centres you. It really feels like the medicine of our times, as it toughens you up and helps you become less reactive to triggers. There's no bullshit with Iboga, they say he is the truth and I believe it! He just gives it to you straight up.

Having said that, not everyone gets Iboga, I'd say roughly for a third of people who try it, it will change their life, another third will reap some rewards and the other third will seem pretty ambiguous and mystified about the whole experience. Some won't get anything at all. Iboga reminds me of one of those underground indie cult bands, you either get his music and he becomes your favourite band of all times, or you don't get him at all and wonder what all the fuss is about.

Ayahuasca can tell you stories that are absolute delusional nonsense at times, but Iboga just lays it down for you in very brutal terms and you just have to take it. I really liked this about him though, as there just isn't enough direct truth in the world at the moment. I say 'he' as it appears as a masculine energy to me, but ultimately, I believe the plants are genderless, they just appear as certain genders and archetypes depending on how they interact with the recipient's system.

The changes I reaped from Iboga were so incredibly deep, I felt drawn to share this plant and with the help of my Iboga teacher and another friend, I went on the Iboga path for the next 2-3 years. I was very much convinced I would become an Iboga shaman during these years, just like I had been very much convinced I was going to be an Ayahuasca shaman before that, but somewhere during my Iboga apprenticeship, I healed the part of myself that felt it needed another thing to define itself by.

Iboga helped me find a new level of wholeness, but then during one Iboga circle I suddenly realized that my work with iboga was over for the foreseeable future. I got the message, 'Alright you've healed enough with me, time to walk on your own two feet for a while now.' I spent some time trying to re-orient myself after this abrupt ending to what I thought was my life path. I did a Native American vision quest - a four-day, four-night fast in the wilderness. This was as important as doing the plants, and showed me that I could get to the same place without taking anything, though in a much slower, grounded way without the psychedelic fireworks.

During the quest I had a visionary dream involving San Pedro cactus, so I reacquainting myself with that medicine and began serving that. It was nice to work with San Pedro after the psychic washing machine of Iboga and Ayahuasca, because it tended to be gentler. Having said that, one or two people always seemed to have an exorcism at my San

Pedro circles so I do not underestimate the power of this medicine, it just seems you have more choice with San Pedro.

As long as you take a full dose, the other medicines almost force you to go deep whether you like it or not, but San Pedro usually leaves it up to you, how deep you wish to go, so I find it a very good introductory medicine for first timers as you always know who and where you are. It's a good benchmark to see how someone might react to something more ego-destroying like Ayahuasca.

San Pedro is a community medicine. It helps people heal relationally with one another, bringing people's triggers to the surface to look at. It is very heart opening and can help you tune into your own heart, which a lot of people are cut off from. Instead of giving direct messages, San Pedro teaches you to tune into your own gut and heart.

The teachings from San Pedro are always practical and reliable, perhaps out of all of the plants (aside from Iboga). San Pedro is very alkaline and has anti-parasitic properties so it is physically cleansing to the gut and seems to help activate the solar plexus. It connects you to nature and the spirits of the land. You can talk to plants, rocks and animals just as our indigenous ancestors once did.

San Pedro is a great couples medicine. I've seen it help people with relationship issues. I know it's helped me heal some of my attachment wounds when I take it with my girlfriend. It's a good medicine for teaching men how to be in a healthy masculine and for women trying to heal wounds from the masculine (Iboga is good for that too).

All the medicines have pros and cons and people will respond more to some over others. It's good to explore until you find the one that you connect with - but know that this can change. Some medicines are also much more sustainable, being easier to grow or obtain than others, so it's important to be flexible during these uncertain times. For example, mushrooms and cactus are easily wild-harvested or cultivated, while Iboga and Ayahuasca take much longer to grow and are often poached from dwindling wild stocks.

I'm not as personally invested in the medicines now. Before, I fully gave myself over to them, almost like I was their servant, but nowadays I don't give all my power up to them. Ultimately, I'm learning that I am the power, invested in me by Spirit, and the medicines are just great friends, teachers and allies that I just happen to be a good bridge for. There are other ways of healing and plant medicines aren't the only way. They have their own set of dangers, traps and limitations and it's important to know these well, otherwise you can get stuck in a loop.

I used to want to save the world and heal everyone but there's no shortage of sick people in the world wanting help. At the end of the day, I need to put myself first. My time as a facilitator recently came to a close in a very natural way. I took several months off and suddenly realized I was reluctant to return. Running groups constantly takes a lot of time and energy. It is an intensive job and role to undertake and I was a bit burned out by it all. I went pretty hard for five years straight. Now everything has come full circle and my energies are being re-directed back towards my creative pursuits. I'm currently writing a comedy show about healing and the plant medicine path.

I'm feeling guided to become more of an educator now. The only way to manifest mass scale consciousness change is for the majority of people who suffer from the standard level of dysfunction to start taking psychedelic healing into their own hands - with some level of guidance and education and a supportive community to check in with. People are doing it anyway!

Communal information sharing about the spaces you can potentially go, will make psychedelic self-healing a more effective and safer process. Unless you have serious trauma, severe mental or physical illness (in which case it's better to seek experienced help), I think it's empowering to take your healing process into your own hands, instead of outsourcing it to an authority, be that a shaman, facilitator, psychotherapist or psychiatrist. Taking ownership of the process can be the core essence of your own healing.

From my experience, it's best to commit to only one or two medicines at any one time for longer periods, with breaks between to let your system settle. I spent 18 months in a monogamous relationship with Iboga, before committing to the cactus for seven months after taking a long break. If you mix too many, it gets confusing and has the potential to make you crazy and delusional. Your energy can get very messy.

I've facilitated around 2000 individual experiences with Ayahuasca, Kambo, Iboga and San Pedro - around 300 circles of varying sizes, which is nothing compared to some of my contemporaries, but I have a good idea of the territory and have seen many healing miracles. I wish I had written them all down so I could remember them all.

One of the most extraordinary healings I saw, was a man with an inoperable brain tumour behind his right eye. After five treatments with Acacia and Syrian rue and Acacia Ayahuasca, the tumour not only stopped growing but completely disappeared. I witnessed one woman with eight years of chronic pain and neuro-fibromyalgia cured in one night with Ayahuasca. She was over the moon, as the illness had ruled her life up until then. Both people had intense emotional releases which cemented my belief in the psychosomatic origins of some illnesses from unprocessed emotions/trauma.

With the Iboga work, I have seen two victims of satanic ritual abuse basically become free of the symptoms of probably the most extreme form of trauma there is. I've also seen Iboga completely eradicate one case of chronic rheumatoid arthritis and a case of treatment resistant partial paralysis of the arm. I've seen Iboga microdosing over an extended period neurologically reset chronic methamphetamine abusers. They literally went from being paranoid delusional to having relatively normal lives again.

Because these medicines are so powerful, there are dangers and risks involved. Over the years I've encountered a handful of experiences that really made me question the medicine work and informed the way I did things. Probably the most negative experience I had was with a client who did not tell me that he had been in ER with cardiac issues a few days prior to the circle. Before the circles I ask people if they've taken any substances or had any health issues that I should know about, but he failed to mention it because he was so eager to be a part of the circle. My previous 20 circles had been very calm and peaceful, so I think I wasn't as careful in reading the signs. I ended up having to call an ambulance when his breathing became erratic.

I then found out from his wife afterwards that he had been very sick in the leadup. This really damaged my trust in people after that and I had to tighten my screening process. I got PTSD from that experience and had to clear it with Ayahuasca. I learnt a lot about my people-pleasing tendencies from this. In hindsight there were red flags that I overlooked, mainly because the past 20 ceremonies had gone so well.

I wasn't going to let him sit, but he begged to be a part of the ceremony and I felt for him, so I served him some mushrooms instead of Ayahuasca. I let him stay, and this is what happened! I thought mushrooms were quite safe and he'd tried a large dose before, but these were Psilocybe subaeruginosa which can induce a syndrome called 'wood lover's paralysis' as we both discovered that night.

One of the biggest problems with this work is that people often can't own, or handle what comes up for them in the ceremony, because they are so shut down, they don't know what's inside them in the first place. Then suddenly they are in the thick of it for several hours and there is no way out. They can flip out, try to leave the ceremony or project their crap onto you. You have to be as clear and non-reactive as possible.

My one fear about the mainstreaming of plant medicines is that people have no idea what they are getting into. There are levels to this work that just do not fit into the Western materialist paradigm. It does not include the spiritual paradigm whatsoever and some illnesses - for example, certain addictions and mental health issues are spiritual illnesses in my opinion. I'm worried corporate interests are going to get involved and interfere with the purity of the medicine. You can see that happening already to some extent. Big business is getting involved and co-opting the medicines in order to become a money-spinning affair.

The other issue is that a lot of illnesses are systemic in origin. It's the system we're trapped in that makes people sick. Corporatization of the plants means that they might become another band-aid to help a malignant, unsustainable system continue running until manmade environmental collapse. Western medicine is great for some health issues but it's very mechanistic and in some ways, just an extension of the very system that is making people sick. Incorporating sacred plant medicines into this pre-existing system of disconnection just seems problematic on an essential base level.

Missing from the mainstream dialogue is all the incredibly weird shit that can happen on these medicines. There are spiritual realms that they access that the Western paradigm has no knowledge of and will write off as a hallucination or worse - pathology. Encounters with spirits, entities, ancestors, deities and so on, will be downplayed. In indigenous traditions, these experiences are the focal point and have a lot to do with the healing. In fact, one of the best ways these medicines can heal you is opening you up to a higher spiritual and supernatural dimension. The scientific materialist paradigm that basically posits us as a random occurrence on a rock, floating in dead space, is somewhat of a depressing downer. Suddenly remembering all the magic in the universe that you once accepted without question as a child is terrifically healing.

Ceremony is always filled with synchronicities, bizarre coincidences, and mystical experiences. A lot of this is subjective and hard to prove scientifically but I've had many encounters with all sorts of spirits and entities that seem like something out of a fantasy or sci-fi novel. Sometimes these things can be a distraction from the deeper work taking place. The real test is how such encounters affect the person and how they are in the world when the medicine wears off. If it makes you are a better and more functional person in the world then fantastic – if not, then perhaps you are experience chasing.

The way things are happening in the West is haphazard - a lot of people self-initiating. After some years in the scene, I can see that it's a very random process and there's such a thing as a failed or incomplete initiation that can cause all sorts of problems, increased addiction tendencies, spiritual bypassing, ego inflation, mental health issues, energetic system imbalance and more. This is why we need to pool our resources and try to map this territory and then spread this information to those who walk this path. Here in the West, we are all working it out ourselves. There are certain risks as we attempt to rebuild bridges back to what our culture has lost, whether you follow a lineage or the DIY path. I've met enough casualties in the scene. It is a trial-and-error process as we try to map this new (yet ancient) terrain in relation to the contemporary world.

The plant path is a greatly accelerated path so the ups and downs tend to be more intense and while the highs have been great, some of the lows I have had to experience, I wouldn't wish on anyone. The more light you experience, the more shadow gets dredged up, so it's a constant swing between two poles. Research into the yogic and Taoist paths, spiritual emergence and Bill Plotkin's work on soul initiation and soul descent has been invaluable in helping me frame and understand the process that I and many others have been going through with these medicines and the times we are in.

Indigenous plant medicine practices, have purification rituals that are done first, but here in the West, some people just fly to the top of the mountain without using these processes. I believe complications can happen this way. We will likely see more of this as the movement expands. We have no system of approved elders to oversee and guide the self-initiation process, so it can be more hazardous. According to Arnold van Gennep there are three phases to initiation: Normality - Initiation - Return. A huge part of the initiation process is returning as a new person, often with a new name and a new set of responsibilities, but in this day and age this does not happen.

If you come back from experiencing God, talking to nature or entering deeply altered states, modern society rejects you and categorises you as mentally ill. As difficult as the self-initiation process is, this is the way it's supposed to happen in the West, as we are no longer indigenous peoples. We need to find new ways and novel methods suited to our westernized psyches that the medicine can adapt to, in the most effective manner. I see this phase as the start of many new syncretic Western lineages, though not all are going to make it in the end.

If you are considering facilitating, you probably won't listen to me and go do it your own way anyway. That was me at least! I recommend doing as much of your own healing as possible first, but it's also hard to say this, because we are living on borrowed time with where the world is at politically, societally and environmentally and time is of the essence. We are in a bottleneck at the moment and perhaps there is between 5-15 years left before we face multiple levels of systemic collapse. Perhaps it's all hands-on deck and let the cards fall as they may. Though one big mistake that I made, was to bring my own wounds into the work early on. I didn't realise it in the beginning - I only noticed as I healed more.

You need to check your intention constantly. Where does your need to help come from? There can be both altruistic and personal motives to doing this work and it changes all the time. You might resonate with someone's struggle because it's a reflection of your own, and without knowing it, you subconsciously believe that if you heal them, you will heal yourself. You can get too close. Stuff like that.

You must be vigilant of both yourself and others. The ego is very tricky and can get ahead of itself. You can become too attached to working with the plants and over-identify with the work and the role. This is dangerous because you can lose perspective. It's wise to take long breaks, just to take stock. I haven't drunk Ayahuasca for two years and that really helped me integrate the five years of intensive Ayahuasca work I did prior to that.

It's important to have healthy boundaries with both yourself and clients. Be very clear with them. And get ready to be projected upon - both negatively and positively. I've been accused of being both Satan and Jesus several times now. People will also project their parental or familial stuff onto you. It's important to learn to be non-reactive and not take anything on that isn't yours. Whoever triggers you, just indicates the cracks in your shell that need looking into.

It's easy to become a cult-leader in this job and you must be very wary of when social politics become a thing, it happens easily without you even knowing. If twenty people are telling you how great you are all the time and everyone is on medicine, including yourself, eventually it will go to your head. Taking regular breaks from the medicine is helpful to check in with baseline consciousness, otherwise you can get warped.

I've had to watch the line between healing and enabling. People still have room for bypassing or these medicines and it can become too recreational or surface level in its effect. You can actually use the medicine to avoid facing your demons, and get stuck in a superficial experience-chasing loop that you mistake as healing. Those with a history of addiction can use it as a perceived healthier alternative to getting messed up. I prefer working with people who have done a lot of work on themselves and are driven to heal. By the end, I was over working with psychonauts and experience chasers. It doesn't seem worth the hassle and I don't want to help people to escape themselves.

If you want to do this work, prepare to go through many difficult trials. Not only are you breaking the law but you are also opening up cans of worms in people's psyches and there will be consequences. If you want a peaceful life, go do something else! Don't get me wrong, I love what serving the medicine has taught me, but there have been some testing periods where I really wanted to give up and do something else. It's not easy and you are continually tested and shown your weak spots. You need to get over yourself. While you may be further along the path - no one would be paying you hundreds or thousands of dollars to listen to your new age music playlist if there was no medicine involved!

To people seeking a plant medicine practitioner, find someone who knows the lay of the land. Follow your gut. Try to meet them beforehand in person. They should have very clear eyes with few shadows in them. Find good teachers, people who have lived a lot of life, who have experienced much then don't be afraid to test them. Lineage or no-lineage, there are good and bad practitioners of both stripes, but the most important thing is to have a good personal connection with them and that they seem genuine. If you don't trust them on a gut level, then best wait till the right person comes along.

I have tried doing the medicine with purification practices and also without, and I have to say that the cleaner the body, the deeper you go and the safer it seems to be. I really do trust that all these indigenous traditions must have something in them, otherwise why would every single one across the globe stress purification before going into these spaces?

Take regular breaks and do other forms of healing. When combined with plant medicine, they accelerate each other immeasurably. If you rely on medicines too much, they become a crutch and your legs get weak. Last year I took minimal medicine, and mostly did work like: vision quest, tantra, martial arts, qi gong, psychotherapy, ritual, meditation, fasting etc. In many ways it was deeper than medicine alone, because I had to do the work myself.

I think the way forward is to combine both sober work and medicine work in a measured way, along with integration in between. We are living in unprecedented times when all the worlds spiritual traditions, healing modalities and plant medicines are suddenly available to us all at the same time, to be combined in completely novel and unseen ways, so this kind of multi-tradition experimentation is inevitable. People who have already done years of self-work in other modalities have an advantage working with the plants over those who haven't. They take the medicine and their healing process gets turbo charged and they are able to integrate it more effectively.

Don't take every message you receive on the medicine literally. There are ways to read the messages that aren't immediately obvious and I had to learn this the hard way. Sometimes you get direct messages, but other times it's a reflection of your ego and needs to be interpreted more like a dream. Have a good community of people to support you through this process. You need to check in with like-minded people who are going through similar things. Don't check in with people who have no idea what you are talking about because they will think you are crazy!

Don't give your power over to the plants or the shaman. In the end all these beings are helping you, but you are doing the work, it's you that got to the temple in the end, so don't sell yourself short.

Integration is really important. If you aren't living the healings then they haven't been embodied and it's just an intellectual experience. Body work and embodiment practices have been so important for my medicine journey as they helped me integrate and anchor the shifts in my nervous system on a physical and energetic level. You can also get stuck in a pattern of taking medicines way too often. I know this well, because I was stuck for a couple of years. You can end up going around in circles or going a bit crazy. I also got stuck on this idea that I needed to take something all the time to get somewhere. They definitely help, but I do think in the end you are meant to become the medicine and not have to rely on the plants as much, if at all.

Whether you choose the traditional route or self-initiation it's up to the individual. There are pros and cons to each approach. If you find a good teacher and lineage, I think it's much safer that way. Although it is said that if you make it through the DIY process by yourself, you will be stronger and more powerful than anyone working within a lineage.

Aside from getting busted, the main fear I had about facilitating was that someone would have a really negative reaction to it, either physically or mentally. The ambulance experience really shook me and made me reassess how I do things and how much I can actually trust people to be transparent. How I would do things now compared to when I first started, is totally different; more grounded and professional, with tighter screening.

If I am totally honest, in my seven years of service, there were a handful of people that I didn't have the skills, level of healing, or experience at the time, to hold them through their journey. These were mostly in the first 3-4 years. They weren't injured, but they had very strong experiences that were hard to integrate and this may have scared them off the medicine. I've reflected on these experiences quite a bit because I don't want them to happen again, but it is new territory we are entering here and the amount of people I've helped is far greater.

The underground is changing so much and exploding in so many directions. Some people say we should have some kind of underground regulatory body, but I feel that will bring politics into it and things will get nasty. For all their enlightened posturing, medicine people have some of the biggest egos in the world. Also, just because someone has had formalized training doesn't mean they won't abuse their power. Being trauma-informed is important, as is screening.

Things exploded after COVID. Before it was mostly new-age, spiritual types, subcultural types and people on the healing path who did medicine work with me, but post COVID and Michael Pollan's book, I was treating all sorts: bus drivers, cops, commercial divers, doctors, every man and his dog, some of whom had never even smoked pot. They just heard about it on a podcast or from some celebrity like Prince Harry.

As demand grows, we need to be even more careful - for both the clients and our own safety. There are some people who just shouldn't take the medicine at all - it's not worth the risk. There needs to be more education about what to expect, but it's so hard to explain in words. The medicine really is the red pill in some ways and some people are just not ready for that.

Ultimately, people need to become better educated from trusted sources. A big lesson the medicine hammers home is self-responsibility. So, changing the dynamic from; 'I'm the healer and you're the passive recipient,' this top-down approach - to something more equal, where the person understands that they are healing themselves with the assistance of the facilitator and the plants. The more that people can take charge of their own healing, the better.

There is always big discussion about the indigenous vs western approach to facilitation. I cannot speak about the indigenous approach as I have no direct experience yet. But I've researched a variety of indigenous practices from across the world and there are common themes and practices in regards to purification and shamanic healing. I like the spiritual aspect at the base of indigenous practices. Western facilitation can be too clinical, too intellectual and materialistic. Or it can feel like an extension of drug culture - the line gets blurred between healing and having a crazy psychedelic experience.

We have a lot to learn from indigenous practices, but just because someone is indigenous does not necessarily mean that they own the plants, nor that they are automatically ethical. There is a lot of black magic, charlatans and abuse of power in that world too. It's easy for westerners to be taken advantage of because of our idealization and romanticization of indigenous cultures. While there are some incredible indigenous healers out there, I've also heard plenty of nasty stories about people being exploited because of these illusions. Both approaches have their place and a balance needs to be struck between tried-and-true practices that can be adapted, but not necessarily culturally appropriated, keeping in mind that the culture, psyches and land where these indigenous practices arose from are distinct and different from the people one may be trying to heal and where the healing takes place.

Indigenous plant medicine healing practices arise organically from the bioregion they are endemic to, so it's problematic to just cut and paste them into an entirely new locale thousands of miles away - with plants that aren't endemic to that area. Also, there is the question of cultural appropriation and the danger of using a foreign symbology system that is not what you grew up with. Invoking the jaguar with a Shipibo dialect is not the most natural thing to do when you are in Australia surrounded by Kangaroos.

The strength of the western approach is that it has been created by westerners for westerners, stripped free of unnecessary dogma or superstition. We should try to find the underlying commonalities, practices and mechanisms of the varied indigenous plant medicine healing practices and work on creating a new tradition that is tailored towards healing issues endemic to Western psyches.

For example, most cultures have exorcism rites, smudging rituals, cleansing and purgative rituals. Bring in aspects of Western clinical practice that are really important like; trauma awareness, medical support and intake screening. The most promising models I've seen combine the best of both worlds - shamans and curanderos working alongside western doctors and psychotherapists to create a synthesis of both worlds.

We are still in the wild west phase of medicine work - but the way I see it came to me while observing how an Ayahuasca vine grows. It throws out a hundred different tendrils and branches in every direction and the ones that catch somewhere, begin to proliferate, and grow, becoming huge, strong branches, while the ones that don't gain traction, shrivel up and die. So, right now, we are a hundred different branches being thrown out at once and hopefully, in our lifetime, we will see where each of them leads.

CHAPTER EIGHT

Yvonne S – Kambo.

My journey into the mystical world of plant medicine is guided by a simple but powerful drive: to live my life to the fullest, in every possible way; physically, mentally, and spiritually. My name is Yvonne, and I am a part time plant medicine practitioner. I work simultaneously in both, the plant medicine world and the 'default' world. I have a degree in digital communication, and a corporate career. I own a home, am financially stable, and if you met me in an everyday setting, you would not guess that I am a seasoned psychedelic explorer and a trained Kambo practitioner.

With my contribution to this wonderful book, I aim to make the idea of the 'underground' and plant medicines more accessible to the 'general public.' It's about removing the stigma around psychedelics and stereotypes around plant medicines and Kambo, and provide testament to their benefits. One does not have to be a 'hippy,' living in the hills to embrace plant medicines and be part of this movement.

For as long as I can remember, I have had within me a seeking, a sense of wanting more from life. I've been drawn to the edges of the conventional world, looking to explore what lies beyond. I don't just mean traveling to new places or trying out different hobbies, although I do that as well -

I'm talking about a deep, soul-level craving for experiences that expand my mind, enrich my spirit, and make me a better version of myself. I'm happy to try anything at least once. Combine this yearning with my innate belief and trust in nature's healing abilities, then it's clear that my journey towards ancient remedies has been a natural progression.

My childhood was a happy one, I grew up with my mom, who is a very strong, highly artistic, creative, yet career driven woman. With my mom, I travelled the world; she taught me to love art; introduced me to fine dining; and encouraged grit and persistence. Though, I always felt that mum had very high expectations of me that were sometimes impossible to meet.

My parents split up when I was a toddler. I never had a relationship with my father nor lived with them together again in the same house. I was very attached to mum, and quite anxious. She would often have to come and pick me up before night fall from my friends' houses, although we had organised a sleep over. In hindsight, I believe that growing up without my dad in my life affected me subconsciously, and has influenced how I relate to people. For example, it probably manifested in me staying way too long in a very toxic marriage with my second husband. We brought out the worst in each other, and despite the fact the violence was regular, I didn't leave for a very long time. My need for harmony and peace has always been very strong. I was a big-time people pleaser.

In 2015, I finally extricated myself from my 13-year-long marriage and around the same time, I received an invitation to partake in an Ayahuasca Ceremony. I was already familiar with psychedelics from earlier phases in my life and driven by a need for self-understanding and release of my unhealthy behaviour patterns, I embraced the chance to experience this magical, transformative brew.

My first ayahuasca journey was extremely beautiful. I experienced the deepest unconditional love for myself and compassion for my ex-husband. It vanquished all my pain, sadness, and resentment about this relationship, as I could see him for the wounded person he is. I understood that the behaviours displayed in our relationship were not meant to harm me personally but were a result of his childhood trauma. Coming out of this journey I realised that I had no ill feelings towards him, nor did I hold any grudges. As a result of that we are still friends today.

It was not long after my first Ayahuasca journey that I heard about Kambo; the secretion of the Phyllo-medusa Bicolour Frog, native to South America. At that stage I was quite scared of Kambo. Ayahuasca was portrayed to me as something that might make me nauseous, but it had the other amazing effects that made up for that - the images and deep insights - whereas Kambo was portrayed as just a full-on purgative. The idea of taking some poisonous 'frog goo' to experience such an ordeal was not at all enticing. I politely declined all offers for three solid years.

Meanwhile, I remained committed to my personal growth and healing, immersing myself in a variety of practices like Yoga and Meditation. I studied Reiki and Body Work and began sharing these healing gifts with clients. Being of service to others in the alternative therapy field was deeply fulfilling. It also provided a refreshing balance to my life in a male-dominated corporate world.

I kept journeying with Ayahuasca, during which time, I had a few super intense sessions. One that stands out, is when millions of tiny nanobots from another realm, came and entered my body through every orifice and set about repairing me on a deep cellular level. Physically it was a deep healing process. There was no fear, just complete surrender.

Then three little men in white overalls started scrubbing, my heart out. My heart turned different shades of pink and red as they rinsed their sponges out into big buckets. It was truly amazing.

During the second half of this journey, I got very physically sick and actually thought I was going to die. Nauseous for hours, puking my guts out and sweating profusely, I lay there thinking, I just have to breathe through this, and I'll get to other side. I believe that Ayahusca was working on the trauma I'd experienced during my son's birth. When I went into labour, the hospital realised that he was breach, which resulted in me having a C section (Caesarean). I was quite young, and living in New York when he was born. Having a newborn with no family support felt overwhelming. I also felt cheated and resented not having had a natural childbirth. My nervous system eventually relaxed, after what felt like hours. The next day, I woke crying, happy to be alive, and that feeling of missing out on natural childbirth had completely disappeared!

In a much later and very profound ayahuasca experience, I received a download from the trees. I experienced them swaying in the background, their song lines forming an additional layer in front. I gained a deep knowing that we must protect the trees. It was very emotional and touching and I felt an extreme connection to nature. The song lines looked like the Peruvian Shipibo tapestries not the Aboriginal paintings. The message I received was that; we people are part of nature - just as nature is part of us - everything is interconnected and interdependent on each other, and if we don't take care of nature, humanity will die. From a spiritual perspective, it highlighted the fact that spirit is in everything. I was already quite involved in environmentalism before this, but my ayahuasca experience gave the environmental cause a supercharge and made me even more aware.

Some of my ayahuasca journeys have seemed a bit meaningless, I've even slept through some of them. Often there are no clear revelations or insights at all. Nevertheless, Ayahuasca harmonised me and I experienced subtle, but noticeable changes. I became far more capable of setting healthy boundaries. I started feeling secure and confident in myself and my relationships. I became aware of the power that lies within me. It also became clear that I'm fiercely independent, fearless, and capable of (almost) anything. On the flip side I never ask for help and this habit needs some balancing, if I want to experience love, affection, and kindness in my life.

Things continued to unfold. In 2018, a good friend from New Zealand, who just happened to be a Kambo practitioner, came to Australia. I had gotten to the point where the call to work with Ayahuasca had subsided and I was having a break from it. My friend invited me to join one of his Kambo ceremonies and this time, something felt different and a voice within me whispered, 'you're ready for this.' So, with absolute trust in him, I took the plunge.

In a semi-rural area near Brisbane, we gathered in a tipi, enveloped in nature - with my friend leading the ceremony, five like-minded individuals, embarked on a transformative journey. The minute the Kambo secretion entered my system, a gentle wave of love washed over me - as comforting as a mother's embrace, holding me in warmth and safety. I had a deep sense then that I'd found my medicine.

Kambo had been portrayed to me by other people and the media, as a violent, painful, brush with death—but my experience was quite the opposite; gentle and uplifting. Sure, there was some purging, but it was effortless. The entire process lasted just fifteen minutes.

My first Kambo kiss, rendered me superhuman. My mind was clear - my senses felt supercharged; eyesight, smell, and hearing. My brain fog disappeared. I felt rejuvenated - almost reborn. I also had a big physical shift: allergies that had plagued me for over four decades vanished, and my chronic back pain eased. Emotionally, I felt invincible and serene, in perfect balance, and perfectly at peace. The days following the ceremony my energy levels and mental clarity soared. I found new heights of productivity which was very beneficial to my busy professional and personal life. It seemed amazing how a small application of frog secretion could bring about such transformation.

Medical research into Kambo was spearheaded in the 1980s by Italian researcher, Vittorio Erspammer, (and later picked up by American Scientists) revealed that the secretions of the Phyllo Medusa Bicolour frog contain peptides beneficial to human physiology. The bioactive peptides contained in Kambo serve multiple purposes, from boosting the immune system to deep bodily cleansing. Potent analgesic, antibiotic and antimicrobial properties, effectively neutralise harmful microorganisms and reinforce the immune system. If you are interested in the science of Kambo, there's a plethora of information online.

Indigenous communities in the Amazon have honoured Kambo for centuries, seamlessly blending ancestral wisdom with intuitive healing practices. While science expands our understanding of these potent compounds and most of the identified peptides can be re-created in the lab, it has not been possible to produce something that has the same effect on body, mind, and spirit. To be honest we don't really know how Kambo works, but we know it definitely does something good. A purely reductionist, scientific approach is not sufficient to explain Kambo as it possesses qualities that impact the human body in ways beyond what can be fully understood.

After my first Kambo experience, I immediately felt a strong calling to become a carrier of this medicine. It's difficult to put into words, it was one of those "when you know, you know" scenarios. So, I immersed myself completely into the world of the frog, learning as much as I could. I wanted to share this gift with others, to help them find balance, reach their full potential, and live a life free of suffering.

My practitioner training took place in Northern New South Wales guided by the International Association of Kambo Practitioners, (IAKP) an organisation that has been training practitioners since 2014. The entrance criteria were quite stringent: a minimum of 6 to 10 personal Kambo experiences; solid physical and emotional health and a genuine commitment to the work. Clean health, meaning no serious psychological diagnoses, not any contraindicated medical conditions. Additionally, you are required to complete a first aid course and receive mentorship from an established IAKP practitioner.

The sessions leading up to my training were far more intense than my initial, somewhat blissful encounter. I can attest that sitting with the frog is not always a casual encounter, it demands courage and resolve. Though the benefits were amazing - every time I went in for another one, I asked myself, "What the fuck am I doing?" During the15-day training, I had to face 5 Kambo sessions, three within three hours. However, every second was worth it.

During my mentorship I assisted in the administration of Kambo treatments to clients. I gained technical expertise through both traditional and contemporary methods. The program included comprehensive lectures and education covering all aspects of Kambo application and potential contraindications. Beyond the academic and practical knowledge, it was an intense, transformative journey of self-discovery and personal growth.

This initiation process was quite daunting. The '3 x 3' (three rounds of Kambo in three hours) is intense. One student was the designated recipient, while another was administering it. The dose increased with each round to account for the body's adaption to Kambo's effects. The teacher demonstrated by applying the first round as the student observes. In the second round, the student applied the Kambo under the watchful eye of the teacher. Finally, in the third round, the teacher steps back, allowing the student to assume full control. For the receiving student, this sequence requires a deep level of trust as well as emotional and physical surrender to the process. The aim was to dissolve any residual fears or apprehensions about the Kambo medicine or the ritual itself.

Being on the receiving end of this '3 x 3' was one of the most intense experiences of my life. The only way out was through. It was my biggest lesson in surrender to an extremely uncomfortable process. It was reminiscent of my most harrowing ayahuasca journey. The tight knit community of students and teachers carried me through. During the training process, everyone had to compose a song and my most vivid memory whilst undergoing my third-round ordeal was the group singing my song to me. I felt safe and supported, and very accomplished afterwards. My fellow students and I faced our biggest fear and came out stronger, feeling very enlivened.

During the early stages of my private Kambo practice, the use and supply of Kambo was still legal in Australia. Being part of an international association granted me invaluable resources: ongoing support, safety updates, and information on potential risks and red flags. This international network was bolstered by a community of Kambo practitioners right here in Australia. Through open forums and collaborations, we were able to exchange ideas and work together. We all shared the same hope—that Kambo would remain unregulated, as it is globally, or at least become regulated in a manner that established a code of conduct and framework for safe practice.

Unfortunately, there were a couple of incidents in Australia where Kambo treatments turned fatal. These tragedies were largely caused by practitioner error and neglect (failure to call an ambulance) rather than the Kambo itself. Potential tragedies have also been averted by speedy action from qualified practitioners, which highlights the crucial role of proper training and duty of care.

The decision to ban Kambo in Australia is, in my opinion, short-sighted and dangerous. It drives it into the shadows, making it far riskier. Underground practitioners are cut off from critical safety resources and information. Fear of legal repercussions makes it less likely that people will seek medical help when needed. Worse still, the ban could embolden amateurs to administer Kambo without understanding the contraindications, risks, or safety measures involved. Given the emergence of therapeutic medicines such as medicinal marijuana, MDMA, and psilocybin mushrooms, into mainstream medicine, the decision to ban Kambo is particularly perplexing and counterintuitive to the direction in which things seem to be moving.

I welcome the mainstreaming of plant medicines. It's amazing that Australia has permitted the use of MDMA and psilocybin in clinical settings. While it reduces the stigma of these substances, my concern is that the push towards legalisation is accompanied by corporate interests. While the mainstream acceptance of plant medicines will lead to further research and safer administration, the commercialisation factor will make treatment inaccessible for those who really need them.

Given that plant medicines have deep-rooted traditions in indigenous communities, where they have been used for centuries and considered a communal resource, not a commodity, this is particularly concerning. Will traditional custodians benefit in any way from this commercialisation or will profits be siphoned off by pharmaceutical companies? If we don't balance the need for scientific validation and safety protocols with the need for equitable access and respect for traditional practices, we risk turning valuable therapeutic resources into products for the wealthy, rather than accessible tools for healing.

With this in mind, the underground plays an important role by serving as a counterweight to the commercialisation of plant medicines. While operating in the shadows comes with legal risks, it ensures that treatment remain accessible to a wider range of people.

The underground may also preserve the sacred aspects of these medicines – as all the practitioners I know are aware of the spiritual components, which may be lost in a commercial setting. Most underground practitioners work based on trust, community, and a deep-rooted understanding of healing over massive profits. In my opinion, this leads to a more holistic, compassionate, and personalised treatment. Many are involved in advocacy and educational work, raising awareness about benefits and risks of the medicines, and offering a more nuanced view to the mainstream dialogue. Overall, I think that it is important for people to have multiple channels through which they can access help.

I continue to offer Kambo to existing clients and only accept new clients through trusted referrals. I don't advertise my services. I always conduct a comprehensive assessment to ensure client safety, screening for potential contraindications and also to understand the client's motivations for seeking out Kambo. This potent substance is not suitable for everyone. Occasionally I choose not to work with a client, if my intuition tells me that their motivation isn't aligned with the deeper purpose of Kambo—or if they're just chasing a new thrill, or if I sense that Kambo won't serve their overall well-being.

I have adapted my practice and transitioned to offering "dry" Kambo sessions only. Before Kambo was banned in Australia, I adhered to the traditional "wet" Kambo protocol, which involved a client consuming up to 2 litres of water before the Kambo was administered. This leads to the purging experience that Kambo is infamous for. However, any form of vomiting, carries a risk of oesophageal perforation or rupture, and also called Boerhaave syndrome, which can be a life-threatening condition if not treated promptly. Regrettably, there have been two known instances of this occurring in Kambo ceremonies in Australia. One way of reducing the risk is to not induce a purge at all.

I conduct my sessions in small groups (4 max) as well as one-on-one. The dry method is an impactful experience that offers remarkable transformation. I use small amounts of Kambo to cleanse the system. The ceremony typically comprises multiple rounds, where the client will delve deeply into the process for a couple of minutes and then return to baseline before embarking on the next round. I incorporate other modalities such as; meditation, breathwork (pranayama), and sound healing throughout the ceremony. Dry Kambo is blissful, tranquil, and meditative, albeit subtle and provides the same benefits as wet.

I have witnessed some profound changes and healing in the people I've worked with. For instance, a 48-year-old guy who'd lived with a debilitating form of fibromyalgia for 30 years, wasn't able to work and had tried every traditional treatment possible. After receiving Kambo, he regained energy. It took a few years of Kambo every three months, but now he can hold down a job. I believe that most diseases are psychosomatic, especially auto-immune dis-ease. Fibromyalgia is such a weird thing with its many and varied symptoms including but not limited to: chronic fatigue, chronic pain, and brain fog. Western medicine is great for emergency care, but not always equipped to look at people with chronic dis-ease holistically.

People with no other plant medicine experience will get a big physical detox from Kambo. A rush of heat then nausea and then a big oral and anal purge. People who have had other plant medicines may get a different response. Blocked energy can be released and the emotional body worked on. I've even occasionally found Kambo to be a psychedelic experience - on a big dose. I've even seen fractals.

Some ayahuasca facilitators use Kambo as a preparation, because these substances complement each other beautifully. Cleansing the system first gives ayahuasca a clean slate to work with. Furthermore, Kambo relaxes you, as it attaches to the opioid receptors, reducing the potential fear that comes with embarking on an ayahuasca journey.

Kambo is a huge manifestation tool. Anything I've ever wished for has come through. Maybe it's because I'm generally much healthier and happier but I find that Kambo opens gateways and puts things in place. You can materialise things such as the beautiful home I live in, but also relationships and work opportunities. I swear Kambo played cupid in finding my amazingly supportive and loving partner.

One of the most notable benefits that clients report is a significant downregulation of their nervous system. In an era where anxiety disorders are prolific this is invaluable. My beloved, who was very sceptical of Kambo described experiencing a sense of relaxation, balance, and calm after his first experience. This endured for weeks. Triggers that used to upset him lost potency. He said it was as if he left his dirty washing at the door.

Many clients report a decrease in pain, anxiety, and fatigue, along with improved mood, heightened energy, and an overall enhanced sense of well-being. Drawing from my extensive study of meditation, I recognize the critical role that the relaxation response plays in healing. Kambo serves as an effective tool for achieving this deeply relaxed state that facilitates genuine healing.

If you are interested in having Kambo, it's important to find a qualified practitioner that you feel a genuine connection with, someone who conducts rigorous screening and has expertise in first aid and mental health, to ensure your emotional safety during the experience. Regardless of Kambo's legal status in Australia, they must be prepared to call emergency services should a medical crisis occur. The Kambo should come from trusted supplier and be ethically sourced, for both environmental sustainability and quality of the medicine.

For anyone interested in facilitating Kambo, comprehensive training is essential. It should encompass traditional practices as well as Western adaptations. While it's tempting to train directly with tribes in the Peruvian jungle, these communities often lack insight into Western health issues and may not provide the most applicable training for a such a clientele.

Australia stands alone in its legal stance against Kambo; being the only country where both supply and usage are outlawed. For those residing outside Australia, it's important to know your local laws as they may differ. Various reputable training organizations operate globally and can be found online.

I feel deeply attuned to the spirit of Kambo and capable of managing both my own energy and that of my clients. I am not a "shaman"—my role isn't to "fix" or judge. My primary responsibility is to provide a supportive, safe environment for transformative growth. I am forever grateful to the spirit of the frog for the healing, insight, clarity, love, compassion, strength, courage, and balance it has brought into my life. May the frogs always be happy, healthy, and free, may the tribes who protect the forest always be happy, healthy, and free, and may those, who need the gift of the frog be free to access it safely.

My last words on the underground – while my personal experience in the underground has always been very positive and I've felt well cared for and safe, I'm haunted by the poor guy who recently passed away after receiving Kambo. This could have been avoided had someone bothered to call an ambulance. We don't need cowboys and this behaviour just can't happen. It endangers the medicine, the underground, and the clients. Facilitators must embrace a duty of care and a willingness to do the right thing despite legal implications.

CHAPTER NINE

Alex Korjavine – Kambo, Changa, Ayahuasca, Cactus

Born in Russia, I moved to Australia in 1998. Upon arrival I worked as a commercial cleaner and security guard, not really stimulating employment but I made a good living out of it. By 2006 I was a head of security for Balmoral Beach Club and living in Mosman. As an avid kayaker and mountaineer, I spread my time between work, travel, and sports pursuits.

My interest in plant medicines began in 2009, after taking LSD and discovering its magical properties. My main reason for starting this work was a healthy dose of curiosity. I started learning more about plants that had similar qualities, mainly the ones that abound in South America and are a part of intrinsic cultural heritage of many South American tribes.

At that time, Peru was an obvious go-to destination for me, due to travel programmes I'd seen on TV and some of the late Alan Shoemaker, ayahuasca related posts (RIP) on emerging social media platforms. So, in March 2010, I booked my ticket to Peru. It was long journey filled with adventures that included a trip to Galapagos Islands, and mountain biking from the volcano Cotopaxi.

One of the highlights was meeting Lesley Myburgh, (known as La Gringa), a well-known San Pedro facilitator living in Cusco. She served me my first San Pedro cactus at her place near the Temple of the Moon in the Andes. I stood gazing at the Andes with waves of San Pedro flowing through me, and had a clear feeling that I'd discovered the holy grail. It was similar to LSD in many ways but with much more loving and heart opening energy. It was incredible.

Two days later I flew to Puerto Maldonado where I drank my first cup of Ayahuasca with a curandero apprenticed to Don Bechin, a well-known curandero in these parts. It was magic – that first cup. Even after consuming hundreds of cups in the last thirteen years, I remember this ceremony as one of the most life changing experiences of my life.

When that first cup was served, one of the male participants, actually knelt down on the ground, before taking his cup. I smirked - it looked a bit too sanctimonious to me, to kneel down in front of a cup of some drink. Hundreds of LSD trips had made me quite cocky. I drank mine standing up and then sat down. When the world started to change, I understood why the man had knelt down - it is right to kneel in the presence of higher powers. And the powers that catapulted me into this colour infused vortex and void, were too powerful to simply be knelt in front of. When the second cup was served, I crawled up to the curandero and fully prostrated myself before him. If the dictionary needed an illustration of the word 'humbled,' I was it.

After a few years of visiting (mainly Shipibo) curanderos I decided to learn about the broader aspect of it all. Anthropology and history were always strong interests of mine so I hoped to discover how the ayahuasca vine was incorporated into other Amazonian cultures. I realised that the main focus laid within the Shipibo culture, but in reality, the Ayahuasca vine is present in lots of places; Colombia, Ecuador and Brazil. And so came my first trip to Colombia in 2014.

I made contact with a curandera from the Inga tribe; Donna Marta Queroz Burgos and with her I drank the first of many cups that would turn into numerous visits over the next four years, as well as an apprenticeship in her ancestral homeland of the Putumayo.

What surprised me was how different the cultures of drinking and brewing the Banisteriopsis Caapi vine were. In Columbia it is considered a male spirit not a female spirit as is perpetuated in Shipibo myths. The Inga and Cofan tribes believe that the female spirit comes from the Chacruna (not the vine) and that the sacred Yage brew is actually a marriage of the two. The brewing methods were quite different from the Shipibo. A lot more care is used in the preparation of the vine – as in the hand maceration with mallets into a pulp as compared to just using whole pieces of vine as seen in some villages around Iquitos.

During these times, I had absolutely no idea about the existence of Australian Medicine circles. I got connected to these purely by chance, during one of my Colombian trips which also coincided with my first Changa experience. Donna Marta told me that one of her guests had left her some smokable stuff that, according to him, worked like ayahuasca. She'd never bothered trying it, since she believed working with ayahuasca alone was enough, but she was curious to see its effects.

'Queres probar?' she asked; 'Si senora,' I replied. She produced some brownish tobacco mix. With nothing to use as a pipe, I looked around and my eyes settled on a middle-sized carrot. My mom had always made carrot roses on top of the salad so I knew how malleable they are. So, with the use of a screwdriver and a knife I managed to MacGyver myself a decent looking pipe.

There I was sitting in a kitchen of my Curandera, with a carrot and a lighter in my hands ready to blast off on my first Changa experience. Since I had not tried it before I had no idea about correct dosage - but let's say I had a carrot-full. After having drunk ayahuasca for some time now, I had full respect for its power, but I did not feel the same about this strange looking novelty mix left by some crazy Brazilian guy. So wrong. So very wrong!

My first thought, just seconds after inhaling it was, 'Fuck me, what have I done. I've just killed myself. The second thought was 'How sad' and then the darkness and endless spins. I remember vividly that at some point I started seeing very colourful, multi coloured bands that appeared out of darkness allowing me to grab them. The sudden relief was palpable. They pulled me through the ink of the universe. I was going to survive this on these bands of magic. Seconds or minutes later, the realisation came that what I'd perceived as colourful bands were actually sounds of guitar chords.

When I opened my eyes, in front of me, was a girl with a guitar and she was singing a song - Spiral by Darpan. The girl's name was Andrea and she had her own retreat centre in Costa Rica. She had come to brew some ayahuasca. I asked her about what just happened and she said that she knew I needed some help and thought that this song would be perfect. We spent the few remaining days talking, brewing medicine and playing guitar. I used to play but had lost interest for a while. But now, I was bursting with music.

Two weeks later, on my birthday, I received another Darpan song in my email box from Andrea, as a birthday gift. I was wondering why this name kept popping up all the time and too my amazement the universe provided just one hour later. Just below her link to the song in my email box was an invitation to participate in an Ayahuasca ceremony in the Blue Mountains, NSW, and the facilitators name was Darpan!

So that's how my Australian medicine journey started. Since then, I've met many wonderful people who are a part of the Australian Psychedelic landscape. But I will always remember the day that Darpan invited me to sing at that ceremony. I found my voice and my purpose. I decided that I would serve this medicine one day and bring along the vibrations and the music.

SAN PEDRO

After my experiences with Lesley Myburgh, I became interested in San Pedro. I started to grow it on the balcony of my Mosman flat in 2014. I am amazed at the cactus's resilience and strength - it barely needs any water or care and becomes more potent with stress. Once I left a foot sized chunk of cactus in a cupboard and forgot about it for year. Upon its discovery, it was white from lack of light, but still perfectly healthy. Two pups were growing from one side and roots on the other. No soil. No light. No water. I successfully replanted it and ate a big chunk of it the following year. What a powerhouse of withstanding and stoicism!

I learned of San Pedro's power to treat addiction from my friends in the Andes. Cactus works by gently showing the way - like a good grandfather. It may be a stern grandfather at times, but it's always loving and caring. Having Russian and Ukrainian heritage, I know many people who suffer from generations of alcohol abuse and are only too happy to break this cycle. And so, I gave San Pedro to some of my alcoholic friends and the results were great. It manifested in most either completely stopping their alcohol consumption or developing a healthier relationship with it and significant reduction in use. Being a phenethylamine, San Pedro is closely related to MDMA - it works well for trauma and entrenched fear in a similar way.

ACACIA

I drank an Acacia brew for the first time at one of Darpan's circles but never really paid any attention to it, as my studies were mainly focused on the Colombian Taita Yage culture at that time. My interest was sparked when I went to a lecture given by Julian Palmer in a Bondi Cafe in 2016. We slowly became friends and Julian shared a lot of his wisdom and magic about the Australian Acacias and his invention, 'Changa.' Later on, I started serving Acacia brews combined with the ayahuasca vine, I got from the jungle. It had a crisp visionary quality and uncompromising power.

KAMBO

As everything seems to be synchronous and connected, I first heard of Kambo in 2014, during the first night of Darpan's memorable retreat. I had bunked in the same room as a medicine musician who was playing at the ceremony. His name was Themis, and he told me about the magical Frog ceremony that made your will strong, silenced the internal dialogue and killed procrastination.

Kambo came to my attention several times again over the next few years but only in name and the occasional story from friends. At that time the Kambo movement was still in its infancy. There was the occasional visit by some South American Kambo facilitators but that was once in blue moon. Finally, I was invited by my dear friend, Simon Robinson, to a Kambo ceremony held by Louise, the one and only Australian member of the mysterious and very closed organisation called IAKP - a newly formed International Association of Kambo Practitioners based in England and led by Karen Kanya Dark.

There were twenty-five members and the waiting list for training was several months. Luckily, I was invited to play medicine music at a retreat held by Karen in NSW. We immediately hit it off and shared many interesting conversations. She agreed to open up a space for me in the next training scheduled for August 2016 in Poland. It was a two-week intensive course of daily training and regular Kambo applications.

Upon my return to Australia, I had many medicine friends waiting to try Kambo and that's how it started: first a few relatives, then a few friends and then it just snowballed. Most people came with psychological problems but a few were seeking self-empowerment. By the end of 2016, I was seeing ten to fifteen people a week. I called my house in Neutral Bay, 'Casa de Sapo' and started a Facebook group called, 'Green Light of the Frog' where sessions were advertised every weekend. It was like throwing a rock in the water and watching the circles expand. People who'd experienced Kambo would bring friends and relatives - moms would bring children and children would bring parents, some even wanted to bring their pets! The power of the Frog was undeniable.

I also started serving Kambo as a guest facilitator at a variety of retreats. But I did most of my work from a wonderful garden space, below a house that smelled like tons of sage had been burnt there over the years and had the undeniable air of a place that had seen some pretty weird stuff. It was the site of many transformations and healing experiences, thousands of emptied purge buckets, but most importantly, learning.

I was privileged to serve some of the major psychedelic players their first Kambo experience, and many other interesting people. I've served nurses from intensive care - to help them focus and fight stress and fatigue, business people to push their agenda in board rooms, people with psoriasis and arthritis, people with fear of public speaking, alcoholics and coke fiends, traumatised sexual abuse survivors, sports people who needed discipline to train better and win, and a huge number of people that just needed a little dose of confidence in their daily life. Many clients have become my friends.

In the over 2500 sessions that I've conducted from 2016 till 2020, I've watched the interest in Kambo peak. IAKP hold dozens of training courses around the world and train hundreds of practitioners. I was an assistant teacher in 2017 with the Australian IAKP. We eventually parted ways due to some differences in opinion in how Kambo worked and methods of practice. While I still respect the training I received, I work differently and do not adhere to their rigid structure. I pushed for more scientific research to be done on Kambo peptides, but noticed a clear lack of interest from IAKP management at that time.

2018 bought an important turning point in my life - it was time to give back. After finding out that I'd been serving the Frog medicine, my Colombian friends who had taught me so much about the mysteries of Ayahuasca, were interested in learning about Kambo. The Putumayo lies in higher territory than the habitat of the Kambo frog. It was a great honour to share with my teachers, a healing modality that was not a part of their cultural heritage, but a significant part of their Peruvian and Brazilian neighbour's culture. The irony of the universe and its mysterious ways - a Russian guy, living in Australia, introducing Peruvian medicine to Colombian curanderos - weirder things have happened.

On that fateful trip, I introduced Kambo to Juan Carlos Torres, a Colombian writer. He eventually wrote about his experiences with Ayahuasca, San Pedro, Iboga and Kambo in a book called, 'Soy Buho,' (I am the Owl) published in 2020. I was privileged to be mentioned in his novel. We met again this year at Donna Marta's 73rd birthday – and I received my long-awaited, signed copy.

Unfortunately, due to a few tragic malpractices that lead to some Kambo fatalities, the Australian Health Board, in a knee jerk response, banned Kambo in October 2021. They gave it a Schedule 10, regulatory level. (Heroin and cocaine are only Schedule 9.) Possession, sale and usage are now prohibited in Australia – making it the only country in the world where Kambo is illegal.

So now, I only serve Kambo overseas where interest is steadily growing. In order to obtain Kambo, I've built great relationships with various communities of the Matses tribes that live along the Amazon and Ucayali River - most of whom live primitive lives and lack education. We recently returned from a trip to the Amazon where we delivered books and school supplies to the children of Communidad Ibama. We also help support various Matses tribe community projects - from funding medical supplies to boat repairs.

MEDICINE MUSIC

I have always believed in power of vibration to alter a humans' frequency. Certain sounds, both vocal and instrumental can affect us on both an emotional and physiological level. So, the decision to employ music as my helper while working with plant medicines, came easily. Most of my mother's family are very musical - my great grandmother was a piano teacher and my grandpa, an amateur jazz musician with a crazy sense of rhythm. He playing drums in local jazz bands in the 60s. My mom and aunt both played piano and sang - so family gatherings were filled with the sounds of piano and accordion. Dad, however was almost tone death and managed to spoil any song with his usually drunken baritone. My grandmother tutored me in the piano. I taught myself guitar and sang in a choir. Despite my love of music, I never learned to read it – I learned to play guitar by watching a video repeatedly.

The musician I met at Darpan's Ayahuasca retreat was a great inspiration and a lot of plant medicine inspired synchronicities paved the way. I invited him to my house, where I served him with his first ever Cactus. What ensued was 14 hours of playing music, impromptu recordings and discussions. He was musical genius, with the voice of an angel. It was so androgynous that when you listened with your eyes closed, it was impossible to tell his gender. He played every type of string instrument and flute known to man. He could play anything, anywhere. His enthusiasm for music and discipline in practising was so infectious that I carried this with me through the years.

In my last nine years, as part of the Australian Plant Medicine scene and music community, I've learned lots of songs and written a few as well. Music is an intrinsic part of my work. I drink medicine and a day later, I'll learn to play a song or give birth to one of my own. I play both live and recorded music during ceremonies. It is soothing to hear the vibration of a human voice while journeying and also very healing. I can usually predict what emotional response a song or composition will have on a circle during a certain moment in ceremony. And sometimes when the medicine is particularly strong, it matters not what instrument is played; they all make the space pulsate with pure energy.

I experienced what channelling music meant, when it emerged from my mouth as a flowing energy vortex, coming out in a variety of forms and shapes, sometimes colourful, sometimes invisible but still clearly tangible. It often surprises me how effortless the process of singing is - just breath in, breath out and let the medicine sing through. That's what singing on Ayahuasca feels like.

I vividly remember a ceremony on the Central Coast, led by a well-known Brazilian. I was a helper, musician and Kambo facilitator. The songs were coming in such a strong wave that I lost all understanding of the guitar chords and milliseconds later had forgotten the lyrics too. I felt dissociated but could hear that my fingers were playing amazingly well. The biggest shock came when I heard someone singing perfectly - in a voice strong and deep and carrying the vibration of the medicine song perfectly to the circle. It was my voice! I kept singing without being aware of it. It was utterly shocking for me to realise, that for a period in time, I was not in full control of my body, yet still performing tasks such as playing and singing. States like this are attainable on Ayahuasca – though can't be replicated consciously with effort or training. In fact, the magic disappears as soon as the conscious mind enters the stage and tries to take the microphone from MADRE ayahuasca.

CYPRESS HILL.

At the end of 2017, after spending a couple of years as a musician for Brazilian Ciranda Circles (a Santo Daime offshoot) I started gathering my own groups at a remote property in the Hunter Valley. I called it 'The Cypress Hill Retreat.' I held monthly groups there and also rented it to other facilitators. Many of my Aussie friends reading this book will probably have had some wild experiences there. It's an incredible piece of land with Mt Dangar standing as sentinel in front of the property. A giant, pyramid shaped mountain looms over the black, pine covered land. Two locally quarried stone cottages and forty acres of peace and quiet - so remote that the previous owner said that only God and he knew of its location. The beauty of a location like Cypress Hill is that participants can have a cathartic release and scream their lungs out, without drawing the attention of police or neighbours. The remoteness and sheer space of the grounds are also conducive to the meditative states that ensue after Ayahuasca.

I conduct groups and solo sessions. Most come through word of the mouth as well as my advertising on social media. I have a mailing list and do a mail-out for large retreats. Assessment is done by way of questionnaire. I provide information about the modalities that I work with and contraindications. In the case of Ayahuasca, that's SSRI's and some diagnosed mental health disorders; schizophrenia, psychosis etc. Kambo's contraindications are much broader. The boundaries I set between myself and clients are no sexual interactions or sexual energy of any kind from either side. Secondly, I do not serve medicine to people who have been coerced by relatives or friends. You must want it yourself.

While working with ayahuasca, the closest I came to an initiation was during a ceremony with Donna Martha in 2014, in Putumayo. It consisted of a daytime Ayahuasca ceremony where all my tools, amulets and top shirt were hung outside the Maloka in the sun and icaros were sung at them for the duration of ceremony. This was done to protect my energy field while brewing medicine and make my tools cleaner and more useful.

My Kambo initiation was more physical and in line with the traditional concept of an initiation. Usually, a Kambo ceremony consists of single application of certain number of dots and lasts 30 minutes. During the initiation this amount triples. After the first application the initiate rests for 30 minutes and then another Kambo application is applied with an increased number of dots. Then the process repeats again. Overall, the initiation lasts 3 hours and involves lots of purging. The concept behind the ordeal is so that the initiate can see that the body can take pretty much any amount of Kambo without harm, if the procedure is done correctly and the recipient has no contraindications. I have received 33 points of Kambo in 3 hours - first 9, then 11 and then 13.

I believe that in order to facilitate the medicine a person needs a certain skill set. First, an intricate knowledge of the substance they are using; chemical composition, interactions with other substances and potential for harm. They need to be abreast of new developments and research happening in the field. They must be able to communicate clearly and understand the client's needs and purpose for attending. Being a good listener is important. A facilitator who works with plants that alter human perception must be solid and grounded - and must combine their acquired knowledge with calm self-assurance. No one wants a practitioner who is disorganised or unsure, nor one who is sad or emotionally unbalanced.

People considering taking part in plant or animal medicine sessions need to do extensive research. Don't just believe your potential facilitator - ask questions and beware of practitioners who don't give clear answers and use cliches. This usually indicates a lack of experience and may be dangerous. This work is too important to not understand things like human anatomy and chemical interactions.

Both indigenous and western knowledge are important. Tradition and acquired wisdom combined with modern technology and research makes the whole package somewhat safer. For example, in the indigenous use of Kambo, little attention is paid to the physical contraindications. Anyone can receive Kambo, and I've seen babies a few months old given it as a vaccine. Most tribes live remotely, with few schools and little education.

There is no one better than a Matses tribesman to tell you; where to find the frog, how to call it, when Kambo is at its strongest and in season, what to do to relieve someone's suffering during a powerful Kambo session, and how to call in the forest spirits. But tribal knowledge on contemporary diseases, contraindications, and chemical interactions is limited.

There was a fatal case in Brazil, where a man with an enlarged heart died during a Kambo ceremony, led by a member of the Katukina tribe. A heart condition would be contraindicated in IAKP training manuals, so with proper assessment this participant would have been refused treatment.

The same goes for Ayahuasca, and Australia is a perfect example. Due to an abundance of DMT containing flora, Aussies are pioneers of a changing tradition - entering similar realms but with a different key. Of course, there are traditions of using Mimosa Hostillis in Brazil, but they represent a very small percentage of South American curanderismo in which the traditional Caapi Vine and Chacruna predominate. But in Australia, most ceremonies are held using Acacias. Barely anybody uses Chacruna with the exception of the Santo Daime groups.

The invention of Changa is another example of combining traditional knowledge with current extraction technologies and ethnobotany. Both Acacia and Changa are examples of a modern approach to healing and therapy without taking away the legacy of tradition. I often hear the purist and somewhat ignorant approach to western facilitation from relative newcomers. It usually comes in form of the snobby line; "I only drink ayahuasca with real Shamans in Iquitos." And that stagnant approach has proven erroneous on many historical occasions, because traditions are fluid and subject to evolution even after thousands of years.

A good example is Yopo. This tradition of using 5-MEO-DMT and bufotenine containing beans (Anadanthera Cabrerana), goes back almost 4000 years, according to archaeologists. The oldest finds are pipes in which the remains of Anadanthera beans, indicate a smoking method of use that lasted till 1000 BC. And here is the interesting part. Somewhere around that time, the tradition of smoking the beans changed to insufflating a mix of beans and ash, now known as Yopo.

I'm sure that through trial and error some pioneer realised that this was a more effective way of getting the alkaloids into your system. But I'm also sure that when he brought his new invention to the bean pipe, smoking elders, he was likely ridiculed for shunning traditional ways. Nevertheless, since the period starting 1000BC, only specific pipes for insufflation of Yopo, were found but none for smoking the beans. One tradition effectively transformed into another after 3000 years.

My main concern for the mainstreaming and growing popularity of natural medicines such as Ayahuasca and Kambo is the increased number of facilitators that have no training or experience or deeper knowledge of these modalities. It's the charlatans shining hour now. There's also a growing conflict between medical and mental health practitioners and the underground.

In 2020, I was on a 3-day river cruise in Europe and seated at the dinner table next to a surgeon from a leading European hospital. He showed interest in Kambo and we spent a few days filled with interesting discussions on Kambo's healing properties - its peptide composition and application for a variety of diseases. Originally sceptical, every night he'd retire to his cabin to research Kambo. By the conclusion of the cruise, he was convinced that it was a legitimate therapy with great healing potential. But his farewell phrase, thrown as joke was something that left an aftertaste. He said, 'Alex, do you understand that you are grazing in our field?'

And that's where the concern lies. In the case of Kambo in Australia, we experienced practitioners were squeezed out through illegalization. The upcoming moves to legalise plant medicines will make this field the sole property of the medical establishment and this regulatory approach and the likely price tag will deny healing to those most in need.

Healing always starts with hope. Curt Richter, a researcher at John Hopkins, tested behaviour in mice by having them tread water in a bucket until they gave up and started to drown. When the mice gave up, they were lifted from the water, held for a while then put back in the bucket. Miraculously, they were able to swim for much longer periods of time. Richter concluded that the mice started to drown, not from exhaustion, but from hopelessness, and the act of saving them and introducing hope, dramatically increased their survival time.

Many humans are in the same situation - hopelessly treading water with no hope of change in their monotonous, trauma ridden lives. The plant medicine experience can be that miracle - the Curt Richter hand, that pulls a person out of the grind of his seemingly predictable life, even for a short period of time, showing that other possibilities lay beyond. Where individuals have hope they have much higher levels of perseverance and resilience.

AYAHUASCA

I've witnessed so many great results while working with Ayahuasca. It contributes to healing the soul with its ability to access hidden memories and bring them to the surface. It can give a person a different outlook on their traumatic experiences, achieve catharsis and heal.

Not only traumatic memories are revealed, but good ones too. One notable example was a female client who had a serious issue with parental love. She was at a crossroads in her life and feeling alienated from her family. She could not figure out if it was due to her own actions of isolating, or an actual lack of love from her family. This issue was giving her anxiety, sleep issues and burgeoning depression.

During her session she started laughing hysterically then crying profusely. I asked what the tears were about. 'Tears of happiness,' she said. The medicine had shown her, herself in a crib as a baby. Her mother, father and older sister were leaning over the crib, looking at her with such adoration that the thought they did NOT love her, seemed ridiculous. They adored and cherished her.

I later overheard her in the kitchen, talking to her mother on the phone and tearfully telling her how much she loved her. She had her phone on speaker mode so I could hear her mother crying on the other end, saying over and over like a mantra; 'We love you so much honey.' Amazingly, a three-decade old, 30 second memory snippet, revealed by the medicine, became the catalyst for this wave of love that broke through the prison of self-isolation and misery.

CHANGA

Changa is incredible tool for accessing other realms and deeper levels of consciousness. It allows more flexibility for both client and facilitator due to its short duration. It has a lot of the same attributes as Ayahuasca but with an immediate and intense onset. The results can be astonishingly quick and powerful too. Sessions are always private as opposed to groups. I offer Changa 3 times during the session. After inhaling the contents of the balloon, the client lays down with eyes closed. Special music is played. Usually, the client is motionless but occasionally may move their hands and feet and roll around depending on the intensity.

Changa usually attracts people looking for guidance who use plant medicines as tools, to access information, get inspiration or answers – the pot of gold that lies at the end of a psychedelic experience. Some come out of curiosity, but there is a steady stream who come to alleviate depression and anxiety. Some are working with a therapist but wish to hasten their progress with psychedelics. Others find traditional therapy unsuccessful and want to try a different approach.

Here is an example of how therapeutic Changa can be. A European woman came to me in 2018. She arrived in state of complete despair, due to the recent and tragic loss of her husband. The manner in which he died was a big part of her issue. During a drunken argument he'd climbed onto their window ledge and pretended he was going to jump. Eventually, he accidently slipped on the edge and fell nine stories to his death. The reason I say eventually, is because she caught him by the hand at the last moment and held onto him for almost two minutes looking into his pleading eyes and hearing him beg her not to let him go. I am sure those 2-minutes must have felt like an eternity.

After hearing her story, I decided to serve her Changa. Immediately after she finished her balloon, her expressionless face lit up with a bright smile. Her eyes moved rapidly behind closed eyelids. She started to breathe deeply and loudly, then laughed and yelled, "They're all there - HE IS THERE." I asked her later what she'd seen and she said that the best way she could describe it was - a waiting room full of souls and her husband was there. She clearly felt that this was not the final place but a halfway station. A preparation room for a larger journey.

The medicine catapulted her to a place where she was able to meet the soul of her husband and communicate with him. She left transformed, with a bright smile and upright posture. We later spoke and she said that this experience was her first step in letting go and continuing to live. She has successfully remarried but keeps fond memories of her previous husband.

My good friend, a Buddhist Monk, tried both Changa and Ayahuasca with me. He believes that plant medicines can give access to the Bardo (the state of souls between death and rebirth.) The ancient Buddhist Yogi's were modern day biohackers who could break into their own physiological system using special techniques to access states unavailable to mere mortals.

The idea of some yogi practicing for years in a cave and learning how to raise endogenous DMT to a level sufficient to open the doors to other realms, does not seem too farfetched. This possibly inspired the concept of, 'The Bardo,' and 'The Tibetan Book of the Dead,' and other ancient teachings. But for one grief-stricken woman, Changa was a doorway to a place where she could say a final good bye to a man she loved.

Plant medicine work is steeped in the supernatural. A lot can be explained by science, physiology and human anatomy, but there's a lot that can't be rationalized. I call it the Grande Mysteria (Big Mystery.) Sometimes these experiences and subsequent results go far beyond our understanding of rational human physiology. I've both witnessed this and experienced it on many occasions.

CHAPTER TEN

Dale C - Psilocybin and MDMA.

An aching desire to heal my debilitating PTSD symptoms led me to worship at the plant medicine altar on bended and bloodied knees. All previous efforts had failed to fully address my trauma and relieve my PTSD symptoms and I'd pretty much tried it all: years of psychotherapy, workshops, spirituality, religion, prescription meds and sobriety. I was pretty much ready to check on out of this life.

When ayahuasca started calling me loud and clear, I'd been abstinent from all drugs and alcohol and in a 12-step program for the previous 17 years. Ayahuasca infiltrated my thoughts and dreams so that I thought about it constantly. I listened to Podcasts, and YouTubes, read books and articles. I joined an Ayahuasca Facebook group eager to learn more and find "the others." It took three more years, before I actually consumed the sacrament, mainly because I feared the judgement and abandonment of my longtime recovery friends. Consuming a non-prescribed, mind-altering substance is considered a relapse in A.A. But ayahuasca doesn't care about that and doesn't give up easily. Thank God.

Camped out on the bottom rung of life's emotional ladder with nowhere left to turn, I'd pretty much surrendered to a self-inflicted death when Grace reached out a slender hand of pity - a synchronistic introduction to an Aussie Ayahuasca facilitator from a guy in the Ayahuasca, Facebook group. I checked Julian out and the green light was given - so I flew to Oz in early 2017 to take part in my first two Ayahuasca ceremonies.

Let me just say emphatically that drinking ayahuasca is no walk in the park and it's sure not for the faint of heart. Intense, confronting, and paradigm shattering, it's a true and profound initiation. The person who enters that particular cave is not the same one who returns.

This dark bitter brew of vine and tree awoke me from a deep amnestic sleep. I retrieved missing pieces of myself; my memory and my soul. It totally rocked my world. I relived traumatic events from my childhood in confrontational technicolor - fully experiencing; emotionally, somatically, spiritually, and intellectually, the immense abandonment, shame and despair I'd felt as a child, growing up at the hands of an ex-military, dictator.

I was shown how my shame kept me separated and isolated from others and how the intense physical, sexual and emotional abuse I'd received, resulted in my extreme lack of trust in people. I simultaneously witnessed these events from both a child and adult perspective. I saw how my child self, had interpreted events as if they were her fault. I felt her intense despair as she lost faith in a God who didn't protect her – how she felt so overwhelmed that she did not want to be here on this earth. And somehow in the experiencing of all of this, my heavy sack of PTSD symptoms pretty much disappeared. Don't get me wrong, I still had work to do, but my ayahuasca initiation both saved and upgraded my life.

Let me just say that when you have endured years of suffering and navigated a maze of dead-end therapy doorways – when you've stood on the precipice ready to jump - then you find profound and instant healing in a 2-night ayahuasca ceremony, it simply can't be ignored. When something this monumental, smacks you in the face, it wakes you up and begs your attention – and there is simply no walking away.

I knew I had to move to Oz. I was onto something incredibly special and although I didn't know it at the time - what was to become my destiny. Over the next few years, synchronicity led me on a magical mystery tour. I attended ayahuasca ceremonies with various facilitators, with the intention to both heal and learn. I was introduced to other plant medicines: cactus, mushrooms and Kambo. I helped out at ceremonies with various facilitators. I was taught how to find, identify and pick a special acacia and how to make the brew. Then one day, as payment for helping at an ayahuasca ceremony, I was given a small quantity of pure MDMA.

I'd never had MDMA before but I quickly discovered that this is the kiss of life and true golden key for healing PTSD, without the re-traumatization that can occur with plant medicines. An entactogen made in a lab, pure MDMA has the amazing ability to crack your subconscious wide open and elicit repressed memories, going right back to being a toddler in a cot. A true heart medicine and supremely effective in the right set and setting for healing trauma. And when I say pure, I mean pure, not ecstasy pills that most people associate with MDMA. Those pills contain about 10% MDMA if you're lucky. And I must emphasise that there's a vast difference taking MDMA in a therapeutic container than using it recreationally.

My motivation for providing underground psychedelic therapy is simply this; I know what it's like to suffer and did so for many years. I know for certain that talk therapy, which operates on a cerebral, intellectual, head level, will simply not touch the sides of PTSD - this deeply entrenched program that needs a cataclysmic shift - the shift that only psychedelics can provide.

The abject despair of living with PTSD cannot be understated. It manifests in hypervigilance, nightmares, flashbacks and dissociation. The sufferer is triggered by many things, which makes their behavior seem over the top. They can be aggressive, quick to flare up and defensive – they may act and feel like a child. But knowing all this on an intellectual level, simply won't stop it. They are incapable of changing these primal responses, that emerge from deep within their psyche -so, they watch in despair as jobs, friendships and relationships all go west. This eventually plunges them into a deep well of despair until suicide seems the only viable option.

Just two ayahuasca sessions rid me of most of these symptoms. So yes, despite the illegality, I feel morally compelled to help others achieve the same freedom that I have. Functional mental health is a fundamental human right. So, despite the illegality of this work, my conscience is utterly clear. The law against psychedelics is an ass and a breach of human rights. When I started out, sure, I was afraid of getting caught, and proceeded very cautiously - but then I'd get an email from a client, telling me how this therapy had saved their life - and that just kind of sealed my fate.

These laws are unjust and as a civilized society we should feel compelled to either change them or ignore them. Adults have a sovereign right to do what they like with their own bodies, as long as they are of sound mind and truly understand the implications. Shakespeare said, 'To thine own self be true,' and despite the potential repercussions, I choose to answer to a higher source and my internal moral code.

My clients have included police, war veterans and first responders. Many were psychologists and therapists - too afraid to break the law themselves, they came to me for their own treatment first and then referred their clients. The bulk of my clients were survivors of childhood sexual abuse - territory I understand very well. Many were professionals, including; university lecturers, veterinarians, lawyers, architects, and doctors.

Prior to all this, in what feels like another lifetime now, I worked as an addiction counsellor, specializing in benzodiazepine addiction and detoxification. I have a degree in psychology and am a certified addiction counsellor. Based on my own experience of navigating the Australian underground, I saw a real need for someone who was trauma informed to step up. Most of the facilitators I'd encountered, although well-meaning had no idea how to work with a traumatised person - nor did they have much knowledge of addiction.

Giving people profound and paradigm shattering medicines then leaving them alone to process all the repressed stuff that emerges, is certainly not ideal. It is important to do a proper assessment before providing medicine to ensure that the recipient will be safe. It is important to prepare clients for this intensely challenging work. They should have access to follow up integration counselling, if it is needed. Things have moved on a bit from the late teens when I started – there are now more people wearing the 'trauma informed' badge, though I am not sure how much of this is accurate or true.

Ayahuasca was the first medicine I served because this was the one, I started with. It all went very well for a while, but in time it proved a wild and gnarly medicine to work with. After a particularly harrowing event, I felt out of my league with this medicine and moved on to work exclusively with psilocybin and MDMA. These are far easier to facilitate, more predictable, yet still extremely effective for healing trauma. Ayahuasca needs the right environment - somewhere quiet, out in nature, where people can let loose – and they often do. It also requires a massive amount of training and experience.

The results for most clients have been profound - lifesaving in some cases. But it's important to state that not everyone experiences a remarkable transformation, despite all the mainstream media hype and rhetoric. These medicines are not for everyone. Having conducted hundreds of solo sessions over the years, I've learned a lot. These are tertiary medicines so I believe clients need to have done a good deal of previous self-development work. People in active addiction won't gain optimal long-term benefit unless they embark on some course of mindful self-inquiry or addiction recovery. I often encourage such people to get time up in a 12-step program before even thinking of doing plant medicine work.

Psychedelics are not magic bullets for everything but they work extremely well for PTSD, and such clients notice an immediate reduction in symptoms. People with addiction issues may get a good head start but they usually need to make lifestyle changes or they will eventually resort to familiar behaviors. For example, they may need to change their playmates, playthings, and playgrounds - end a toxic relationship, leave a job, change self-sabotaging behaviors, including but not limited to diet and health. I usually avoid giving MDMA to addiction prone clients - particularly those in recovery as it feels good and hence is more likely to unleash the beast of addiction. Mushrooms are often a safer bet.

People with "genuine ADHD" won't respond well to MDMA as this medicine just won't work. Drugs like Ritalin are amphetamines and act like speed for most people, but has a paradoxical (opposite) effect on people with ADHD (it slows them down.) I say "genuine ADHD" as many people are wrongly diagnosed... part of Big Pharma's mission to get everyone on prescription drugs.

There are so many positive stories from clients: relief from triggers and hypervigilance are standard fare; anxiety and OCD, gone in one session; depression and suicidal ideation diminished massively; sleep issues resolved, including; nightmares, sleep paralysis, and insomnia; marriages restored; physical pain relieved... the list goes on.

The unconscious holds the key - it holds all our repressed traumatic memories and unconscious programming. These are retrievable with psychedelics. As Carl Jung famously said; "Until you make the unconscious conscious, it will direct your life and you will call it fate." This is profoundly accurate.

One particularly memorable session was with a young, female doctor who had become so debilitated by anxiety, that she had to quit her job at a busy hospital. One ayahuasca session later, she pretty much lost her anxiety and was able to return to work. Her ayahuasca journey was extremely challenging. She relived her birth - and as she was born with the umbilical cord wrapped around her neck, she struggled to breath and communicate and truly thought she was dying. This birth trauma proved to be the root cause of her anxiety. Now how would she ever have discovered that, using conventional therapy?

Another client who had been violently attacked in a Melbourne alleyway while out looking for his missing wife. (She was at the time a recovering alcoholic who had started relapsing after the covid lockdowns.) Immediately after his attack, back in the motel room, he found himself cowering under a table - frantically worried about his wife, not the actual attack he had just experienced.

His MDMA session took him back to a being a 9-year-old boy, cowered under the table at his family home. He had encouraged his younger brother to get up on a garage roof to retrieve a ball they'd been playing with. His brother fell off the roof, landing on his head on the concrete and was knocked unconscious. The frantic parents rushed him to the hospital, leaving my 9-year-old client at home alone for several hours. He spent much of this time cowered under the table terrified, in the dark, thinking his brother was dead and blaming himself. He also felt abandoned, not knowing when his parents would return. His wife going missing had somehow triggered the same feelings and response. At the time he didn't understand why he was reacting this way as he'd forgotten this earlier event – but it all made sense after his MDMA treatment.

Despite the media hype that seems invested in painting a one-sided and glowing version of psychedelics, it's important to state that on occasion things can devolve – especially with, but not limited to, ayahuasca. Those considering becoming ayahuasca facilitators should consider this option very carefully.

Ongoing debate abounds about who should or shouldn't serve Ayahuasca. Those who've trained in Peru will staunchly declare that the medicine should only be administered by jungle shamans with ancestral lineage and years of training. While others say that ayahuasca has spoken and stated that her medicine is needed and should be spread far and wide without any cultural baggage. While I respect Shaman's knowledge, wisdom and training, not everyone can journey into the jungle. Covid, mental health issues, finances and fear, limit this option for many - not to mention the numerous reports of sexual assault, robbery, murder, and sorcery conducted by some of the dodgier jungle shamans. The fact is - it's been happening here in Oz for 20 plus years and is not looking like stopping anytime soon. Nature belongs to all (and none), so we should just quit squabbling and help each other out.

Spirits – well yes, they are alive and well in Oz and speak to us through the medicine. They will certainly let you know if you're doing anything wrong. For example, I once did a client mushroom session on Australia Day. It was full of weird energy and resistance and just didn't seem to flow very well. I upped his dose and it still wasn't flowing. I took a small dose myself and the medicine intuitively communicated to me that I shouldn't be holding medicine ceremonies on Australia Day - because it's a day of mourning. It also told me that I should honour the indigenous spirits in my opening prayer. I usually say a Native American, Four Directions prayer - but now incorporate the local spirits as well. So yes, the spirits are alive and well and I feel they are ok with us whiteys doing medicine work - as long as we are sincere and respectful. Mother Nature and the planet need all the help they can get. I've had other weird things happen in sessions - keys going missing and weird electrical disturbances, like a robot vacuum cleaner turning itself on.

The mainstream scientific dialogue rarely mentions anything of a sacred or spiritual nature but these medicines absolutely connect you to Source/God, other dimensions, and Mother Nature. The plants have spirits that talk to you and to work with them productively, its best to have an ongoing and solid relationship with them. It is going to be very interesting when the men in white coats get wind of this, as they inevitably will.

I believe that therapy with psychedelics should occur on an equal footing - similar to 12-step programs, where it's one addict/alkie helping another. We are all in this together - healing from this insane matrix world. Genuine compassion and care are absolute requirements when working with traumatized people. Consider that you are reliving the client's trauma with them as if you were present. I've watched people relive rapes, right down to the bodily movements, sounds and smells. Intuition and telepathy are heightened while on the medicine, so people will sense if you are judgmental, frightened, repulsed.

Following the medicine session, I always send out a follow up integration and research form. I now have hundreds of these invaluable, post session reports. I really encourage other underground facilitators to do the same. This constitutes some of the most valuable qualitative research available and I often wonder why the mainstream are not lining up to get it – or why they rarely include the client experience in their research – as if the client were just a secondary consideration. A number.

The following example from a male client will demonstrate how deep MDMA can go under the right conditions and how important facilitator knowledge and medicine experience is. I have changed identifying details and have the client's written and verbal permission to publish this. TRIGGER WARNING – contains details of sexual abuse.

Date:

Name:

Age: 51

Substance and Dose: MDMA 130mg

How long did the medicine take to come on? Around 45 minutes but I am uncertain about this as I had no sense of time.

Was this your 1st 2nd 3rd session? 1st

Have you been diagnosed with any Mental Health or Addictive Disorder: e.g. Depression, Anxiety, PTSD. *Over 20 years ago I was diagnosed with Cyclothymia but I believe PTSD or C-PTSD are more accurate.*

Have you suffered from a mental health disorder without an official diagnosis? If so describe. *PTSD, general and social anxiety. Periods of depression in childhood, teens and adulthood until my early 30s.*

Have you taken prescription medication for any mental health disorder? (Antidepressants, benzos, painkillers, mood stabilisers) If so; what, when, and for how long. *I have tried many SSRIs, Epilim and Buspirone. None in the last 20 years and usually only used them for 3-6 months as were ineffective.*

Did you come off any of these prescription medications within the 12 months prior to your session: if so - what, how long on, and how long off. *No*

Did you use any recreational drugs or alcohol in the week prior to your session? If so, what, and when? *None.*

Had you experienced Psychedelic Medicines prior to your session? What, when, why? *I microdosed psilocybin in January this year to reduce my anxiety and increase spiritual connection.*

What was your motivation for doing this therapeutic medicine session? *I wanted some healing. I have done a lot of healing methods, therapy over my life and have plenty of insight but not much symptom relief.*

What intention did you set? *I wanted to like myself more, feel safer, sleep better and find it easier to say no.*

In as much detail as possible, describe how you felt during the active effects? *I felt a slow build up and then a powerful whoosh in my brain that created some fear of being out of control that I worked to let go of so I could fully go with the experience. I had lots of body tremors, shaking and twitching as I remembered past trauma experiences, experiences of grief and regret. My hand was often trying to cover my mouth or push away to protect myself when remembering past abuse incidents.*

In as much detail as possible describe your experience. *I saw sexual and physical abuse from my history that I was aware of and many incidents that I have not been conscious of. I saw myself being sexually abused in other incidents by my father - along with being hit and suffocated; I saw myself as a boy in a lot of fear. I also saw myself being abused as a 5–6-year-old boy in a public toilet by a man the community believed was a pedophile; I felt ambivalent about this experience as he was nice to me when he groomed me and it felt good to be liked, wanted, and touched. I saw an incident where an adult female touched my genitals at Kindy. I did not like this. I was unsure if she was trying to help me but it felt wrong and my body armour tightened as she touched me like I was being violated.*

At times I saw my adult-self going back to help my little boy. To push the perpetrators away or to take him with me. I would bring him to my family with my sons and partner...sometimes my mother, grandfather and other relatives were included. I felt a lot of love and gratitude towards these people. I often saw my child self alone, sad and lonely. I wanted to hold him and comfort him, which I did, but we sometimes still felt disconnected.

I remembered times where I had caused emotional pain to former partners and my brothers. Things I have regretted a lot over the years. I apologized and felt peaceful like I let these past partners go. I was remembering a time where I thought that I had abused other children my age as a child but saw that I had not and what we did was normal childhood experimentation without touch from me. This was a relief.

I remembered my friends living and dead and felt grateful and connected with them all. I made peace with my friends who had passed and how I could not save them. I felt connected to my babies that had passed; sad but not overwhelmed.

I felt all these feelings but in less intense ways than I usually feel things; like on some level it was all okay. I often thought of my partner and felt a lot of love towards her and from her. I felt solid and certain that she is the right person for me.

I saw trees and the water and they were letting me know that we are all connected and I am one with them and not alone and apart. That everything is okay.

I tried to stay open to whatever was coming up but did feel myself tighten up in my brain at times until I could remember to let go physically and mentally.

In as much detail as possible describe what insights you gained? *That I am safe and that a lot of the stuff that I used to feel was urgent and so important doesn't seem that way now. That I need and want more space from people in my life to just feel my own experiences. I feel compassion with what I went through and kindness to that inner child part of me; the small boy wearing his orange Charlie Brown t-shirt. I used to feel like a child in my adult* *life and like I was an adult in my childhood abuse experiences so hated myself for not protecting myself; now I see that I couldn't and that freeze, fawn and fold were the ways I kept myself alive and as safe as possible. I do feel sad but maybe a bit disconnected from that sadness so far; I think it will come. I see clearly how important it is for me to just stay with whatever I feel and that I no longer have to be scared of what will come up; that everything is okay and will be okay and that I still have these tendencies to distract into people or the internet. Just stay.*

How did you feel the next day? Did you experience any come down effects? *I have felt peaceful so far. I drive slower and things bother me less like a message from my ex-wife. I have kept twitching and remembering whenever I am still and stop; the old patterns of avoiding through distraction are there but I see them sooner and feel I will rest, pause and contemplate more to hear what my body through the medicine needs to tell me. I can feel the sadness and loneliness under those urges to distract and connect with new people... reminders to feel and connect more deeply with myself, the earth and the people I already have. I have had short sleeps as I wake and twitch and remember more but it all feels okay and what I need right now.*

Have you noticed any positive changes in your behaviour or demeanor? *I have felt much more peaceful. Quite introspective so my partner has felt a bit disconnected from me but I feel more loving and connected when I meditate on the Brahma Viharas and my heart.*

My cravings feel less strong for sugar and fatty food. I am eating less and feel less intense about should and musts regarding food and exercise as well as work and people pleasing.

I feel more connected with my heart chakra and my body generally. It seems easier to notice my physical tension and armouring and to release it and to feel okay with this being an ongoing process; I am not feeling desperate to feel differently. How I am in the now is okay.

Would you take it again? Why/ why not? *Yes. It was helpful. Very helpful and I do feel that there is more to do.*

Would you recommend it to others? *Yes.*

How you feel about the setting and the facilitation? *The setting was comfortable for me. The facilitation helped me feel safe to open and go deep. You seemed to sense what I needed and that I required minimal guidance; that space, but safe proximity helped. The occasional touch from you was helpful and I felt safer and more open knowing about your life and medicine experiences. The commonalities helped me. You felt like a knowledgeable fellow traveler rather than a professional holding onto power and knowledge over me.*

Is there anything else you would like to add? *Thank you.*

I am privileged to witness miraculous healings on a regular basis. On the flip side, I also get to hear many devastating and ugly stories, that can destroy your faith in the human race. I am no stranger to the evil that humanity is capable of. I have needed to learn self-protection, space protection and cleansing techniques.

And this healing we all speak of, what exactly is it. How does one define healing? For people with CPTSD, just having relief from their symptoms feels like massive healing. In my experience, healing occurs in layers, like the peeling back of an onion. It also depends from where you started. People who have been sexually abused as children often have little regard for themselves and their bodies. Many have allowed themselves to be used and abused sexually - some engaging in dangerous, promiscuous, or addictive sexual behaviour or even prostitution. They may need to learn about setting healthy boundaries, self-respect, reclaiming their body, cherishing their soul and body. This may require removing damaging, disrespectful people from their lives and leaving them behind - including family members.

Healing takes time and can be a lifelong mission for some. Developing faith and trust – dropping defenses – developing good intuition - honoring your own uniqueness and standing strong in it. Mastering your ruminating, negative thinking and stopping self-attack or self-abuse. Practicing gratitude, helping others, making amends, taking responsibility for your own behaviour - these are all aspects of healing.

The underground is integral – it is here to stay and will prevail. Not many people can afford $25,000, for 3 legal MDMA sessions in the mainstream. This is not to negate that there are some genuine, passionate, and ethical people operating there. But the underground will prevail and our job is to keep it safe, accountable, and affordable – and I feel we have done a pretty reasonable job so far.

This therapy is not, nor should it be, a long-term relationship, as clients get well and move on. This will also be a whole new paradigm shift for therapists who are used to seeing patients/clients for years on end.

Lastly, I just want to say that Source communicates and heals via many methods. When I listen to NDE's (Near Death Experience reports) it seems that this terrain is very similar to psychedelic experiences. I can now enter profound spiritual spaces through receiving energy healing or doing meditation. Once you open up this portal to other dimensions with plant medicines, access to these territories becomes more permeable. Meditation, sound healing and breathwork can definitely aid in this. It feels that something magical is upon us - something sacred - a profound evolutionary consciousness shift. If you are called to enter, please don't miss this mystical and magical experience as its probably the missing ingredient to your life. Your life will never be the same again – and that's probably a good thing.

Conclusion

The psychedelic horse bolted long ago - and the mainstream are trying desperately to catch it, gag it, blindfold it, shackle it, and reign it in. The underground voices of experience have been shut down, ghosted and ignored not because they are dodgy or shady characters, as I'm sure the stories in this book can attest - but because they are the proverbial elephant in the room of the "2nd psychedelic renaissance" and pose a threat to their bottom line.

Anything that destigmatizes psychedelics and makes them available to a traumatised public has got to be a step in the right direction. However, these treatments must be affordable, safe and accessible to all those in need and from all accounts, so far, this is not looking likely. For traumatised people awaiting relief, unless they are lucky enough to take part in a research trial, the only way currently forward is to find treatment in the underground.

A blatant example of the mainstreams clearly capitalist agenda and lack of human regard was demonstrated by Compass Pathways in 2019. Owned by wealthy married couple, George Goldsmith and Ekaterina Malievskaia, and backed by PayPal founder, Peter Thiel, along with a few other well-healed moguls - this British biotech company was supposedly dedicated to accelerating patient access to psilocybin for treatment-resistant depression, PTSD and anorexia. Compass won the race to patent synthetic psilocybin and sell it to the masses at an astronomical mark-up. They began charging researchers a ridiculous US$7,000 per gram for its FDA-approved monopoly on synthetic psilocybin. Underground psilocybin mushrooms sell at around $10 to $20 a gram, or are practically free if you pick them yourself or grow them. You would have to be blind, deaf, and dumb not to see the absurdity of this. The one saving grace is that they cannot patent natures freely growing, mushrooms.

Compass became the first psychedelic drug company to go public on the U.S. stock exchange, lifting its valuation to US$1 billion. Starting life as a nonprofit, Compass rounded up some of the most highly regarded psychedelic researchers by offering them all expenses paid, lavish trips. They sought to deviously milk them for their social and intellectual capital and gain access to their research, and by so doing, gain legitimacy. Just two years later, Compass transitioned from a nonprofit to a 'for profit' company. All 9 researchers, when interviewed by Quartz, raised concerns about Compass's operating procedures and ethics - mainly their compromising of patient safety for expediency and profit. All 9 turned down contracts to do further work for Compass. (Quartz, Olivia Goldhill, 2018)

I have already heard several firsthand accounts about the handling – or should I say, mishandling of recently legalised Ketamine Therapy. In at least some cases, psychiatrists are not actually providing therapy with their Ketamine, but just handing out monthly take-home supplies. At least one young woman is now seriously addicted to Ketamine because of this practice and a middle-aged man became psychotic and suicidal after his home alone, self-treatment.

Trauma has become a vast and lucrative enterprise. A multitude of self-described experts lay in wait, ready to cash in on your trauma. Mega conferences swamp Facebook advertising, with 40, 'so called'

Trauma experts at a time. (I'm not too sure when Deepak Chopra became a trauma expert!) Call me a skeptic, but it would almost seem that Trauma is being manufactured to feed the ravenous beast of Big Pharma. But the real question to ponder is this; WHY is so little being done to actually STOP trauma from occurring in the first place?

And why has it been so astoundingly difficult, if not impossible, to find effective psychological help within the mainstream system? Based on my previous role as an addiction counsellor specializing in prescription medication addiction and detox, I would hazard a guess that the reason is this; Big Pharma crave your ongoing and massive financial support. There is simply no profit in a cure. Most traumatised people are slaves to a daily cocktail of prescription pills. Depression meds alone are a 17-billion-dollar worldwide industry.

Big Pharma and their tools of trade (psychiatrists and doctors) are responsible for as much, if not more, carnage and addiction as illegal street drug dealers. Their flippant and prolific overprescribing of highly addictive prescription meds; benzodiazepines, antidepressants, and pain killers, to name a few, has led to extensive addiction, misery, and death by overdose. According to the DEA, Fentanyl alone is the leading cause of death in the USA for 18 - to 45-year-olds and is responsible for 70% of all drug overdoses. It is 50 times stronger than heroin and 100 times stronger than Morphine. According to Peter Gotzsche MD, prescription medications are the 3rd leading cause of death after heart disease and cancer.

While Big Pharma and the venture capitalists seek to get their claws into our ancient and sacred plant medicines - history clearly shows that they are highly unlikely to have our best interests at heart. So why should we be expected to blindly trust in the medical and Pharma fraternity to control and dispense these medicines – medicines they previously demonized - medicines that have been freely used by indigenous societies for centuries.

The DSM (Diagnostic and Statistical Manual of Mental Disorders) written and used by psychologists and psychiatrists to diagnose 'mental health disorders,' completely fails to acknowledge that the root cause of most mental disorders is childhood trauma. Sigmund Freud discovered a long time ago that childhood sexual abuse was the common causal factor that lay behind much mental distress. But after threats from his contemporaries (some of whom were perpetrators) he backtracked on his discovery.

The fallout of trauma manifests in a variety of ways; depression, anxiety, addiction, OCD and PTSD to name a few. But once the trauma is elicited and processed through psychedelic therapy, the symptoms of these "diagnoses" mysteriously disappear.

It was encouraging to hear Bessell van de Kolk, a respected trauma expert and recent convert to psychedelic therapy, mention at a recent 'mega trauma conference,' that post psychedelic, the DSM will likely need to be overhauled or extinguished.

From my experiences as both a recipient and practitioner of underground psychedelic medicines, I question whether the healing of trauma can truly take place in clinical, medical spaces, fraught with such history and controversy. While the psychedelic underground is not perfect, our intentions are genuine and stem from a deep core knowing that these medicines not only rapidly heal us, they are also evolutionary in nature and pretty much imperative to the ongoing survival and transformation of our environment and species.

Yes, there are a few dodgy people in the underground, just as there are some good people in the mainstream who have the best of intentions - but until psychedelic medicines are legal, affordable, and available to those in need, the underground will likely remain the best place to find help - providing you carefully research your facilitator.

It is my hope that this book has provided an accurate account of the facilitators you will find in the Australian underground and has armed the reader with enough information to make an informed decision - so if that if they should feel the call to venture forth and drink from the Psychedelic Chalice - their lives will be changed for the better.

References

Books:

Bache Chris: LSD and the Mind of the Universe, Diamonds from Heaven, Park Street Press. Jan 2020

Carruth Dale; Transformations: Healing Trauma with Psychedelic Therapy, 3 Feathers Books, 2022

Gotzsche Peter; Deadly Medicines and Organised Crime - How Big Pharma Has Corrupted Healthcare, Routledge – 1st Edition 2013

Articles, Papers, Documentaries and Websites:

DEA - U.S. Drug Enforcement Agency. 2023.

EGA (Entheogenisis Australia) Website.

Quartz – Olivia Goldhill, Nov 8th, 2018.

Palmer Julian, Contemplations of the Psychedelic Experience, 2023.